T0384055

The Arab Business Code

Judith Hornok

Routledge
Taylor & Francis Group

LONDON AND NEW YORK

First published 2020
by Routledge
2 Park Square, Milton Park, Abingdon, Oxon OX14 4RN

and by Routledge
52 Vanderbilt Avenue, New York, NY 10017

Routledge is an imprint of the Taylor & Francis Group, an informa business

British Library Cataloguing-in-Publication Data
A catalogue record for this book is available from the British Library

Library of Congress Cataloging-in-Publication Data
Names: Hornok, Judith, author.
Title: The Arab business code / Judith Hornok.
Description: Abingdon, Oxon ; New York, NY : Routledge, 2020. | Includes bibliographical references.
Identifiers: LCCN 2019048893 (print) | LCCN 2019048894 (ebook) | ISBN 9780367265021 (hardback) | ISBN 9780429293528 (ebook)
Subjects: LCSH: Business etiquette--Persian Gulf Region. | National characteristics, Persian Gulf States. | Persian Gulf Region--Social life and customs--21st century.
Classification: LCC HF5389.3.P35 H67 2020 (print) | LCC HF5389.3.P35 (ebook) | DDC 395.5/209174927--dc23
LC record available at https://lccn.loc.gov/2019048893
LC ebook record available at https://lccn.loc.gov/2019048894

ISBN: 978-0-367-26502-1 (hbk)
ISBN: 978-0-429-29352-8 (ebk)

Typeset in Giovanni
by Swales & Willis, Exeter, Devon, UK

If you are wondering what the image of the scroll case on the cover depicts, here's the story: Back in the day, when the Arab Gulf was not yet divided into states like Saudi Arabia or the United Arab Emirates, messages were delivered in these scroll cases. The paper with the message was rolled up and placed in this case and sealed. A broken seal meant the message had been read. Even today these cases can be found in the offices of many Arab business people in the Gulf. These days, it's a souvenir of a past they are proud of, but it also serves as a symbol of safety and trust. Go ahead, and break this seal now, so you can explore the depths of the thought processes of Arab business people of the Gulf.

Contents

Foreword: Why I wrote this book   xi
About the illustrations – the Seven Emotional Hinderers   xiii
      Background: how the Emotional Hinderers evolved   xiii
      The curtain is lifted: where to find the seven characters in the book   xiii

CHAPTER 1   Basics of the Arab Business Code   **1**
Your readiness – are you ready to work in the Arab Gulf? Start to
prepare yourself!   1

1.1   Your homework   1
      Relate – Respect – Relationships   2
1.2   Your personal attitude toward the Arab Gulf   4
      Check your mindset!   5
      The survival masterplan   7
1.3   Your professional competence – would an Arab Gulf expert
      recruit you?   10
      The ideal employee in the Gulf Region   10
      Who am I – and how do Arab business people see me?   13
      Strengths and weaknesses analysis with the ABANA strategy   13
      Becoming an ideal international partner for Arab businesses –
         management of expectations   14
      The 5-step program for managing your expectations   19

CHAPTER 2   Finding a partner – the search for the ideal business partner   **23**

2.1   The desired business partner   24
2.2   Falling in love with a picture   25
2.3   Reality check: Arab Business Code   27

CHAPTER 3   Two innovation strategies for the Arab Business Code   **33**

3.1   The FITO technique   33
3.2   The Gas-Shift-Brake technique   36

CHAPTER 4   Three golden rules of the Arab Business Code   **45**

4.1   Golden Rule no. 1 – Chemistry   45

	Key Code 1 – The sixth sense in the Arab Gulf	48
	Key Code 2 – Communicate authentically from the inside out	51
4.2	Golden Rule no. 2 – Family	53
	Key Code 1 – The power of the word "family"	53
	Key Code 2 – The entire Arab Gulf is "one great family"	58
	Key Code 3 – A good reputation comes first	64
4.3	Golden Rule no. 3 – Respect	106
	Key Code 1 – Clarity and truth in communication	107
	Key Code 2 – Use the building blocks of the Arab negotiation culture	112
	Key Code 3 – Long-term commitment and patience	118
	Key Code 4 – Three cultural no-goes	132
CHAPTER 5	**Communication culture with the Arab Business Code**	**137**
5.1	Silence with the Arab Business Code	142
	Benefits of using silence	143
5.2	Small talk with the Arab Business Code	144
	Benefits of small talk	146
	How to master the art of small talk – the first steps	152
5.3	Humor with the Arab Business Code	157
	How to master humor with the Arab Business Code	165
	How to turn failed attempts at humor into opportunities with the Arab Business Code	168
5.4	Active listening with the Arab Business Code	168
	Why "active listening" in the Gulf is so important	170
	What makes listening so challenging?	170
	Three classics of "reading between the lines"	171
5.5	Signs and body language with the Arab Business Code	176
	Understanding the Arab Business Code with today's sign language	177
	Learn to better read body language using the Arab Business Code	177
	The importance of eye contact	180
	Why Arab business people find it hard to say "NO"	182
5.6	Praise with the Arab Business Code	185
	Three techniques of praise	187
	A list of praise	191
5.7	Inquiry with the Arab Business Code	192
	Pushing solutions through inquiries	194
	Acquiring new contracts through inquiries	196
	Successfully carrying out projects in the millions, by asking questions	197

CHAPTER 6   Conclusion: the commitment   **199**

Appendix – More on the Seven Emotional Hinderers when doing
         business in the Arab Gulf and page directory of the characters   205
Acknowledgments   209
About Judith Hornok   211

Foreword

WHY I WROTE THIS BOOK

It all began in 2010. I was sitting with a group of Arab business people from the Gulf. The atmosphere was pleasant and we all trusted each other. Suddenly one of the businessmen spoke up and from the look on his face it was clear something was really troubling him. "It would mean a great deal if international business people understood people from the Arab Gulf better," he explained. "It's often very, very difficult to work together with people from abroad."

This statement made me take notice, because usually Arab business people from the Gulf never criticize anyone in public. They are respectful of others. The Arab businessman's openness offered me an opportunity. I asked him to tell me exactly what he meant.

He must have trusted me, because he continued to speak and really spoke his mind. His stories and experiences with international companies were filled with perceived misunderstandings. But there was also the sad realization that trust between Arab and international business people had, through diverse incidents, begun to "crumble."

The rest of the evening went smoothly, but it sparked a flame of enthusiasm in me. A MISSION! In that moment, I realized I had just been given an assignment – to show people from different countries how to have more empathy and better insights into their Arab business partners from the Gulf!

In the meantime, a lot has happened in the Gulf and the future will also bring many significant changes. But the one constant is the basis of business culture in the Gulf, which stems from its past. That's why this book is timeless and has a lifelong validity.

Many books and papers have been written on the topic of "successful business in the Arab Gulf" – where helpful rules of behavior, cultural differences, and economic reports are pointed out. I, however, have approached the subject from a different angle. By decoding behaviour, I explore how we can improve cross-cultural communication. I've spent many years working with psychiatrists and brain researchers and, together with my team, examining, analyzing and decoding actions and reactions of Arab business people from the Gulf States. I've had discussions lasting many hours, sometimes all day, with business people from around the world, including all the Gulf States. I have studied their "codes" in great detail, conducted a study with practical measures, and summarized them in this book: *The Arab Business Code* (abbreviated as the "ABC").

My book provides the first glimpse into my findings through case studies of successful international companies and Arab business people and offers solutions and techniques. I have tried to write it as simply as possible, because in simplicity lies "the power to notice" and the success that accompanies it.

View this book as a workbook that you can pick up again and again. It should strengthen your social-emotional competency and develop your attentiveness in dealing with Arab business people. Some contents and techniques will already be familiar to you, but we often forget about them in our hectic daily lives – that's why I've included them here.

Try my techniques and see how they work for you, and tell me what you think.

One more thing: some business people from different parts of the world, as well as the Gulf region, have given me permission to use their names. Others will be mentioned in an indirect way, to maintain confidentiality.

Alright, I've talked enough, all that remains is for me to say: I wish you the very best and, of course, lots of successful business with interesting people from the Arab Gulf region. See you soon!

Sincerely, Judith Hornok.

About the illustrations

THE SEVEN EMOTIONAL HINDERERS

I've always thought in pictures – with every emotional action and reaction by a person, I get a glimpse of a "character." This might take the form of a "fit of anger" or an exaggerated aggressive "ego" or the "prejudice" that rises in us often and leads us to categorize people into familiar biases, according to our experiences.

The greatest inspiration for me in creating these characters was the figures in the old Walt Disney style, where the "bad guys" had to struggle with themselves. Every being has different sides and has different modes of acting and reacting. It's always a question of the situation and how strong-willed and disciplined one is in this moment; the ability to give one's emotional perceptions, the "characters," clear directions in situations such as these. I'm thinking, in the case of the character "Relentless Judgment" for example, of directions such as, "Go away, Relentless Judgment! I don't need you! You are only being counterproductive to our cooperation with our Arab business partner!" The same goes for the "Aggressive Inner Critic" in us, as well as for "Paralyzed Fear" and "Incensed Anger Rascal."

I began to analyze emotional impulses that are especially detrimental to doing business in connection with Arab business people of the Gulf and, here too, I have envisioned these "hinderers" as figures or "characters" and a colorful mix of creatures has come into being.

Lift the curtain – where the seven characters in the book can be found

You will find these characters throughout the book, in different situations between international and Arab business people from the Gulf. Three of the Emotional Hinderers are even pictured in illustrations, with key messages You will also find them listed in the Appendix of the book, as well as a list of pages where each character appears.

CHAPTER 1

Basics
of the Arab Business Code

ARE YOU READY TO WORK IN THE ARAB GULF?

While studying the market in the Arab Gulf, I've noticed three particular kinds of behavior distinguishing international business people with long-term success locally: all of them are authentic, they sincerely mean what they say, and they act from the inside out. And, they always manage to balance their actions and reactions. The success factor can be summarized as:

- Be authentic – always!
- Act from the inside out!
- Keep your inner-self balanced!

While reading this book, remember: these three patterns of behavior, or these inner attitudes, will emerge again and again in the most diverse situations.

Now, let's look at how to get ready for your activity in the Gulf region. There's homework to be done, and you must prepare well.

1.1 YOUR HOMEWORK

In undertaking the classic preparatory steps for the Arab Gulf market, such as doing market research, collecting information on the competition and, of course, displaying one hundred per cent of your selling power – how do you present your company and yourself as its manager?

Of course, you need to gather some basic knowledge about the Islamic faith in the Gulf, in order to have lasting business success locally. There's a lot of very good literature on this topic that can help you understand how Muslims behave amongst themselves. I will not address this here. What I'm focusing on in the Gulf is determining the preparatory steps international business people can take to stand out from the competition.

My findings are to watch out for the three Rs: **Relate – Respect – Relationship**. This simply translates as: show the Arab business people you're interested in them and pay them their due respect! That's the way to form an enduring relationship. To reach this goal, I've come up with three different tools you can combine.

Tool 1: Understand the pride of people in the Gulf about their heritage and history

Background: Those familiar with the Arab Gulf know how proud the locals are of their history and ancestors, especially in Saudi Arabia. A certain knowledge of their background is expected of the international counterpart. This demonstrates respect.

Try the following: let's do an exercise here. Can you answer these questions?

- Do you know how long the United Arab Emirates has been a country in its own right?
- Do you know the names of the last four kings of Saudi Arabia and how this country changed under these rulers? And what that meant for the Saudi business structure?
- Do you know why Gulf States cooperate with each other? Which states have strong ties?
- Do you understand the political goals that led to the establishment of the Gulf States?

If you are unable to answer these questions, do a little reading. The background knowledge will give you a competitive edge.

Tool 2: Understand the tribal relationships within the Gulf region

It's all tribal, especially in Saudi Arabia.

Background: It's important to grasp the nature of this tribal structure and how it developed over time. You don't need to know the whole history of the Bedouins. Concentrate on understanding what made the Gulf States great. Who's behind it all? Who made the relevant decisions?

Goal: How to signal understanding to your counterpart in the talks.

CASE STUDY

An international businessman met with a Saudi Arabian business-man in Riyadh. They discussed business; the visitor had already done some research on the Saudi's family. He knew he was deal-ing with a very distinguished family tribe and let that slip into the conversation. The Arab businessman was touched by this consid-eration, pleased that the international businessman had taken the time, in advance, to get to know him. In turn, he spoke very openly, and showed interest in the conversation.

Try this: Take it a step further and do more extensive research. Talk to other international business people who have been working in the Gulf for a long time. Ask them to tell you detailed stories about the people you plan to work with.

By the way, do you know how the Emirate of Abu Dhabi came about, and who Sheikh Zayed ("Papa Zayed") was? Ask about this. This story will bring a smile to the faces of your local partners, and you are sure to hear praise. You will also sense that your counterparts consider it very respectful of you to be fascinated by the story of their country. This goes for all generations of Arab business people in the Gulf.

Tool 3: Get to know the names of the heads of state and most well-known family tribes

Dynamics: Before you set foot in the Gulf, you need to know who's who and who the decision makers are, along with the names of the people in power.

Among the ruling families there are many members who are very active business people and owners of diverse enterprises, banks, tele-communication companies, oil corporations, as well as medium-sized enterprises like spas and restaurants. Be aware that everybody knows everybody, something we will go into in more detail in Chapter 4 (Golden Rule No. 2: Family). If you can make sense of these connec-tions, if you are well informed about who has ties with whom, who can speak on whose behalf, you're in a great position to start having stimulating business talks and negotiations.

CASE STUDY: *A king is not the same as a sheikh*

I remember one international businessman who had a meeting in the Emirates with a local businessman and kept using the term "king." None of us knew exactly to whom he was referring and didn't respond. At some point, the Arab businessman said to him, "Sorry, but we don't have any kings here. We're a sheikhdom."

Something to consider: This was very embarrassing. It soon became apparent that the international businessman hadn't taken the time to learn the basics about the country – it was a sign of disrespect. And there really is no need for it. All this businessman had to do was a little homework ahead of time.

Conclusion: It's helpful to show your interest in your business partner by knowing the following:

- Their history and their names
- Who's who in the Gulf
- How the country is governed politically
- An overview of religion and history – also something about conflicts in the Middle East. This is a very important subject of conversation and can come up whenever you chat to locals. If you don't know anything about it, it shows a lack of respect, and does not come across well.

1.2 YOUR PERSONAL ATTITUDE TOWARD THE ARAB GULF

Unfortunately, many international business people are still unaware that the mental state and personal attitude of managers and co-workers is absolutely crucial for business success in the Gulf. It involves your thoughts about the people from the Gulf, how you see them, your image of them and their country.

Above all, if you are already working there, remember to take care of yourself, balance work with a personal life, it will help you feel more comfortable and maintain a positive attitude without much effort. In this chapter we will introduce two tools. Tool 1 is a mental check that prepares you for your time in the Arab Gulf. Tool 2 is the essential "survival masterplan." These tools will help you find a good balance between your professional and private life. Let's begin with the mental check.

Tool 1: Check your mindset! The personal mental check

CASE STUDY

I'll never forget one of my business lectures at the Princeton Club in New York. In the middle of my talk a man asked me, in a very aggressive tone: "Why should I do business with Arabs? They're all the same – why should I care about them! They all lie, don't work, and treat women badly." He listed a whole array of negative impressions. I listened carefully, stayed calm and tried not to give any counter arguments, even though there were quite a few things I could've said. Then I told him, in all seriousness, and with great respect: "You're absolutely right! This is definitely not a market for you!" The man was speechless. He stared at me in shock. But it's true, this kind of negative attitude is a recipe for failure.

Even today, I'm still convinced of this. Don't get me wrong, there are people who, despite this sort of attitude, still see the potential to be successful in the Arab Gulf market and I would, by no means, discourage them. This mindset is based on an insecurity, stirred up by frightening images in the media. And this often leads to a clear inner resistance, a kind of defense mechanism. That's understandable. But these people continue to be curious. They're still open to new ways of seeing things, willing to understand another point of view. This can be identified in the way a person asks questions. Unlike this man who interrupted my talk so aggressively. His tone made it very clear: "I don't want to deal with Arabs!" No matter how strong the arguments, nothing would have convinced him otherwise. That's why I'm sure there's no way this man could have had lasting success in the Gulf. The people there would have sensed his hostile attitude – be it verbal or nonverbal. We will focus on this subject in "The Sixth Sense" (p. 48).

This is what international business people say:

We flew in a great specialist, an engineer, from Europe to Saudi Arabia. He kept complaining about the Saudis. Had no respect for them. And this was reflected in the meetings – he was always arrogant and patronizing toward them. Of course, the Arab business people noticed this, and it registered with them. – **German businessman. Branch: Automobile Industry.**

What you need to know: Besides a condescending attitude of international business people toward the locals, greed and arrogance are second and third on the list of slipups in the Gulf. If your counterparts sense even a hint of this attitude, or that you don't care for them, they will diplomatically withdraw from the meeting. That's why you need to have a clear idea about your mental state before you go to a meeting with potential Arab business partners.

Let's do a quick mental check on this to find out what your very personal attitude is toward the Arab Gulf and its people and what your current perceptions of the region and its inhabitants are.

Ask yourself the following questions:

- What do I feel when I hear the term "Arab" or "Gulf State"?
- What does it trigger inside of me? Are these pleasant or unpleasant emotions?
- Have I ever had an experience with an Arab business person before?
- What feeling does the memory of this experience prompt? What images come to mind?

Did you try this? It's exciting to see the associations that come up. And, above all, the emotions it generates, the personal perceptions in that moment.

Especially for top managers of companies and corporations, I strongly recommend that you make your employees do a mental check before you send them off to the Gulf. This is a very good and important investment! Particularly if your goal is to work in Saudi Arabia.

This is what international business people say:

Yes, that's very, very important – because what's not on the CV is the mental attitude. That's not something you can read into it, but for me it's the most important thing for this market. – **Ralf Schiffer, German manager. Branch: Industrial Project Development.**

At times, the aggression employees suppressed would suddenly erupt in the middle of a meeting because these employees were simply not mentally suited for this market. And that's not just bad for business and the employee himself, but also hurts the whole company he represents. – **Abdullah Kuzkaya, German manager. Branch: Power Engineering.**

Call to action to companies: Make sure your potential employees undergo a special "filtering process" in your first talks with them, and definitely before you send them off to the Arab Gulf, so you can test their mental starting position. If you notice these employees have an aversion to Arab business people from the Gulf, don't send them there, no matter how qualified they may be in other respects!

Tool 2: Survival masterplan – a survival strategy

Dynamics: There are many countries in the world where you are not "at home" and where it would be good to prepare a survival plan if you want to work there long term. This is a very smart strategy. No matter how independent, adaptable and strong you are, ultimately you belong to another culture with other values and outlooks on life. And here it makes sense to strike a balance and contemplate what you can do, outside of work, for your mental wellbeing. After all, you want to be there for a long time. But, unfortunately, that's not how some companies see it.

CASE STUDY: Lonely burnout – the slow danger of isolation

I remember a female employee of a well-known international company who was sent to Saudi Arabia, to build up and run the office there. She was glowing with enthusiasm and energy and had a positive attitude toward the country and its people. And it was great fun for me and my team to do the introductory seminar on basic behavioral patterns in the Saudi Arabian market with her. She was eager to learn more, open to new ideas, and therefore, very easy to coach.

We suggested a continuation of the training sessions, in order to accompany her long term in the Gulf States and set up a personal "survival masterplan" for her, focusing on the details and how to build up a good local network. But her company didn't want to invest in any more coaching. Also, based on the woman's character, they felt there seemed to be no need for this; everyone was convinced she would quickly, and without much fuss, settle into the culture there. We, my team and I, did not share this opinion. After half a year, I was told that this young woman had suffered from burnout and left the company.

What happened? No matter how great the potential of this woman was – and although her basic character traits were well suited for the job – to stay in the market in Saudi Arabia long term takes more than just getting used to a foreign country with its own particular customs and laws that one can't change. People are human and an unprepared mental attitude will put a spoke in your wheels in the long run.

This is what international business people say:

> *I had an employee in Saudi Arabia, who was single and lived in a studio apartment in Riyadh. After eight months I saw a drop in his motivation. I noticed there were more and more disagreements between him and the locals in the company. I took him aside for a talk and found out that he felt totally isolated in his private life. Except for going to work, he never left his apartment. He spent the whole weekend there, had no friends in the country. He asked me, "Where can you even go?" This set off my alarm bells and I knew I needed to act fast!* – **Ralf Schiffer, German manager. Branch: Industrial Project Development.**

In the best-case scenario, employers will spot the warning signs early on, like the employer in the previous case study. But sometimes they won't. If worse comes to worst, the employees will get sick and withdraw without giving a reason. What's often behind this is an expression of hopelessness. If we dig deeper, we can see that these people, aside from working, were not able to integrate themselves into the community in the Gulf. The consequences are that the company not only loses a valuable worker but upsets the whole team in that region, and the Arab customers who have grown accustomed to this employee.

That's why international business people working in the Gulf have to prepare themselves and find a balance between work and private life and integrate into the community. This is equally true for men and women. So, let's start here – by preparing a "survival masterplan."

Survival masterplan – Step 1

Ask yourself the following questions:

- How am I currently spending my free time?
- What's the best way for me to relax?
- What am I currently doing, besides my job, to attain a healthy physical balance?
- What efforts am I making, other than working, to achieve a healthy mental balance?

As you can see, here you're trying to determine how to balance out your professional life with your free time. Often people forget to think about this. After you've answered these questions, move on to Step 2.

Survival masterplan – Step 2

Consider how to apply your answers to the Gulf region, how you can meet your needs in your new place of residence and work. Now, it's your turn!

This is what international business people suggest:

Sports: *Some people run, others do yoga or breathing exercises. What's important is to keep moving and relieve stress.* – **Jürgen Löschenkohl, Austrian manager. Branch: Furnishing, Design.**

Humor: *You can't take everything so seriously and let it get to you. I've seen people who have had to stop due to heart problems, because they let too many things get to them. You need to find a way to let it all out.* – **German businessman. Branch, Food Industry.**

Afternoon nap: *Taking personal responsibility in this region and allowing yourself a little siesta in the afternoon is very important. Often you have to meet clients at eight in the evening, and at six in the morning you're off again. On top of that comes the heat. You have to know how much your body can take. And take breaks to rest. Otherwise you won't be able to endure this for long.* – **Robert Wiessler, Austrian businessman. Branch: Service and Equipment for Construction Sites.**

Build personal relationships, learn to be alone, and do something good for yourself.

> *Especially when you start working in the Gulf you need to regularly attend events so you can build up a network – from accepting invitations by the local embassy, the chambers of commerce, to going to expat meetings. But also learn to be happy on your own. That's very important.*

Because there are very depressing periods. When there are sandstorms (the equivalent of our November grey weather in Europe) for example, it can affect your disposition. You need to be aware of this. Also know that this mood will pass. However, you need to do something about it. Treat yourself to a meal in the most expensive restaurant. Really spoil yourself and reward yourself for working so hard. – **Werner Piefer, German businessman. Branch: Safety Technology.**

As the saying goes: "God helps those who help themselves." You need to be proactive, pull yourself out of this depressive atmosphere. The Austrian psychiatrist Dr. Reinhard Haller terms it, *knowing that it's temporary.* "You have to view it like driving through a tunnel," Haller suggests, "and knowing that there's a light at the end of it."

Try this: Come up with a list of rewards with everything you've always wanted to do for yourself. And then go through it, point by point. Give it your best shot!

1.3 YOUR PROFESSIONAL COMPETENCE – WOULD AN ARAB GULF EXPERT RECRUIT YOU?

The ideal employee in the Gulf

What criteria do Gulf experts use to recruit employees for this region? Let's take a closer look at markets in Saudi Arabia. What is the perfect mental makeup of future employees in Saudi Arabia? Here are three points to consider:

This is what international business people say:

Point 1: The first impression of the candidate must convey acceptance!

These employees have the attitude: "Yes, I want to do this! I will totally adjust to Saudi Arabia's system with all its rules and laws." They want to make a difference and be active – also in the scope of working in the Arab Gulf. And they're fully open to this. You don't hear them saying. "I have to," but instead. "I'd like to, I can, I definitely want to." One black mark against the candidate is, for example, if during the talk, when the prayer call sounds from the mosque, the candidate reacts by saying: "Not him again . . . " Then it immediately becomes clear to me that this will not work out in the long run. – **Ralf Schiffer, German manager. Branch: Industrial Project Development.**

Point 2: The candidate does not pose a single question on "safety in Saudi Arabia."

Especially for Saudi Arabia these are the perfect candidates! Their characteristics and mindsets are very similar: open for travel, risk takers; they're looking forward to doing something different in their careers. And they're open minded – that's the key. But if the candidate's initial worry is about safety and their first question is: "Where am I going to live? And am I going to be safe there?" then I already know this is not the right candidate for this market. These candidates are just too scared. – **Robert Hofmann, American businessman. Branch: Real Estate.**

Point 3: The candidate thinks long term.

It's crucial not to enter into this with the motivation: I have a contract for 3–5 years. And then start counting the days. The motivation for this position should not be how much money you're earning, just doing the job to buy a house or an apartment. Anyone not interested in the country, its people and culture is certain to fail. **Austrian businessman. Branch: Special Vehicles.**

Call to action for companies: Let's take it a step further, and ask your candidates intense questions such as: What's your plan? Are you in a relationship? How does your partner feel about living in the Gulf? What have the two of you decided to do? Have you ever been abroad, and if so, what experiences did you have? You want an employee who performs at a top level – so you need to be interested in this person!

Another significant factor in the ideal mental makeup of an employee is strong self-confidence, because these people also have to set limits for their local business partners. Of course, with the utmost respect.

The way to an ideal international business partner for Arab companies – evaluate your strengths and weaknesses in negotiations!

For successful business partnerships it's important to recognize who you are, how you act and above all, how you appear to your Arab counterparts. Thus, my tip to you: before entering your first talk or negotiations, evaluate your strengths and weaknesses in negotiating.

This calls to mind a conversation in the bar of a hotel, with a bar worker. Bartenders are known for their insight into human behavior; they have to listen for hours and hours to men and women telling them all kinds of stories, but also chatting about their fears, joys, worries, and their expectations. And it was the subject of expectations that I spoke to the bartender about. She told me that women would often sit across from her, talking about finding "Mr. Right" and the qualities they expected him to have. She added, "And the amazing thing was, they all had similar expectations: he had to be rich, well connected and, of course, well respected. With a strong personality. Someone you could depend on. Honest and trustworthy. Not to mention, a good lover . . . " After hearing their long list of expectations, the bartender would reply, "And what about you? What do you have to offer?" At that point, the room always grew quiet. All at once, they could think of nothing more to say.

People are very similar in their behavior – in every type of relationship. This case study got me thinking and I decided to try an experiment. During my next workshop with international business people, I asked the participants to describe their ideal business partner. "What do you expect of him or her?" This confused quite a few participants and some of them refused to even think about it, arguing, "What does that even have to do with business in the Gulf? It's obvious what we want in an ideal business partner." But I didn't let up. And the answers I finally got were most interesting: "He has to be rich, well connected and, of course, respected by others, with a strong personality, someone I can depend on. Honest. A person I can trust." Some of them added, that if they really could choose their dream business partner, they would immediately go for a sheikh or another member of a ruling or royal family.

It's amazing, right? Many of their statements were similar to those of the women at the bar describing "Mr. Right." To complete my experiment, I asked the ultimate two questions: "And which of the characteristics you have listed, do you yourself possess? What can you offer?" Silence in the room. This got everyone thinking. And I could see the process of self-reflection begin to work in the participants. Suddenly, they were aware of the high expectations they placed on their future Arab counterparts – and they began to consider what they themselves had to offer.

Why should the Arab businessman choose you?

This is a question you need to ask before your first meeting with the Arab business person. And then go through all the criteria, point by point. It starts with the USP – the unique selling point. There are many approaches you may have missed in the beginning. For example, market niches that you never thought of, where you might have something unique to offer, something the competition doesn't have, or can't do or, maybe, just doesn't want to offer.

Who am I – and how do Arab business people see me?

This is what international business people say:

> *Some companies send new export managers into the market. These people are in the Arab Gulf for the first time and sometimes they have no idea about the background of their own company, what countries their company is active in, or who they are working with. But as representatives they need to know their company one hundred per cent. To the last detail. And you need to be totally prepared, before you enter the market. Otherwise, the Arab business people will not take you seriously. –* **Abdullah Kuzkaya, German manager. Branch: Power Engineering.**

Dynamics: Every time you meet with people, you leave your business partner with an impression of yourself – whether you're an employee or the owner of the company. That's why it needs to be clear up front what image you want to convey to your potential business partners? How should they view you?

The first step in this is learning more about yourself. Analyze your strengths, but also try to see where your weaknesses might be in dealing with an Arab business partner. Only then can you get the upper hand in negotiations.

There are many techniques for determining your strength and weaknesses. One of them is the ABANA (Arab Best Alternative to a Negotiated Agreement) strategy.

Strengths and weaknesses analysis with the ABANA technique

For this strategy to work, you have to be prepared to assess yourself. That's easier said than done. But with the inner decision, "I'm ready, I really want to do this!" it should work. Even if it seems unpleasant to, all at once, look more closely at one's weaknesses.

For ABANA, my team and I were inspired by BATNA (Best Alternative to a Negotiated Agreement) developed at Harvard. This approach gives you alternative options in helping the negotiating partners come to an agreement. These options should be taken into consideration in the preparations, so that one can be as flexible as possible in the negotiations.

We applied this line of reasoning and built our ABANA strategies on it. We asked ourselves what needed to happen for someone to have sharp insights into their position and the position of their Arab business partner and thus have a much clearer structure in the talks. It boosts self-confidence and provides security, a great starting point for negotiations.

Some questions from part of the ABANA strategy:

- What are your strengths and weaknesses regarding your Arab counterpart?
- If the potential partner does not choose you, what are your alternatives and options?
- What compromises are you prepared to make to win the partner over? And where are your boundaries?
- Above all: how dependent are you on your Arab business partner? Are there other business partners you might find it exciting to work with?

There are many ways of standing out from the competition.

Becoming an ideal international partner for Arab businesses – manage your expectations!

Expectations management is a requirement for business success. Our expectations are influenced by many things. How you approach them is essential to your business success in the Gulf, because often the wrong expectations, or lack of expectation management, can upset deals between international and Arab business partners, or create problems in developing the project.

Let's take a closer look at what a lack of preparation and bad management of expectations can bring about. Here's an overview of some possible pitfalls:

Pitfall 1

Result: A bad atmosphere in the meeting room and a loss of focus on the business at hand.

What's happening: If you go to the meeting with the local business partner you've worked well with before, in a good mood and with a positive attitude, you're often convinced that, this time too, things will run smoothly. But maybe the businessman is not there when you arrive, and leaves you waiting. Already, this can cause you to become irritated. Then, maybe, the Arab partner senses this anger, which in turn has a negative effect on him. He might ask questions you find aggressive in tone, and for which you haven't prepared the answers.

Something to consider: If you were less convinced, before the meeting, that everything would work out according to your wishes, then you wouldn't have automatically assumed goodwill or a positive reaction. You would've been better prepared and saved yourself some trouble – and prevented, in the worst case, a canceled deal.

Try this: The moment you begin to feel great disappointment think of "Frustrated Expectation." The creature has taken up residence in you and become active. It's one of the characters in the gang of "Emotional Hinderers" (see Appendix: "More on the Seven Emotional Hinderers when doing business in the Arab Gulf and page directory of the characters"). Visualize "Frustrated Expectation." See it as a character. And be aware that the moment has come when "Frustrated Expectation" is beginning to manipulate you. At times like this, the American psychologist Dr. Guy Winch advises you, at that moment, to say to yourself, "This is a good meeting! Not exactly how I expected it, but let's see how it goes, what comes next." Keep repeating this sentence until "Frustrated Expectation" settles down, because, as Dr. Winch explains, "Don't forget – you are buying time from your counterpart. As long as the meeting is not canceled, a lot can happen. You still have a chance to win the deal." Keep that in mind!

But what if you still can't control "Frustrated Expectation"? Then, if worst comes to worst, you'll slip into pitfall 2. And meet another character: "Incensed Anger Rascal."

Pitfall 2

Result: "Incensed Anger Rascal" makes an appearance. This can be compared to the eruption of an inner volcano. It could lead you to completely lose your composure.

Because this kind of conversation climate runs the risk of building up anger within yourself, against the Arab negotiating partner, and with a flood of aggressive thoughts like the bubbling of rising lava, "Incensed Anger Rascal" starts grumbling: "The nerve of this man – who does he think he is? How dare he talk to me in that way. I never imagined he'd be like that!" These thoughts contribute to a negative development of the situation. Through this inner buildup of anger, you lose your focus, namely, that both of you came to the meeting to develop a successful business deal.

What's even worse, what changes in this instant, like the earth's surface changes before an imminent volcanic eruption, is the tone of your voice. It becomes more aggressive. This alters the whole mood in the room. You probably won't be able to, in a respectful way, shift the attention back to the deal.

Pitfall 3

What's happening: Misconceptions about "mutual" business values and procedures.

Result: An incomplete contract for the Arab business person – terms verbally agreed upon at the meeting are not adhered to. The Arab business partner feels like he's not being respected.

In the international world of business what counts is the contract as the written document, the agreement set down and signed on an actual piece of paper. In the Arab business world, however, spoken agreements have the same value as written contracts. And this is where many joint ventures between international business people and locals from the Gulf fail, because both sides are confused about why the other party is not sticking to their business values and well-known procedures. Arab business people have an extremely good "internal archiving system" in their heads. Everything an international business person says is recorded in their memories, to the smallest detail. So, of course they expect their international counterparts to adhere to these verbal agreements.

CASE STUDY

The sales representative of an American enterprise had a very good business talk with an Arab company owner. During the negotiations the American made several promises as a sign of his willingness to cooperate. He noted down all his promises and brought this information back home to his company in the US. There, lawyers got to work on drafting a contract. What the American sales representative and the Arab businessman are then given to read is a contract that does not include their verbal promises. Even the sales representative's request to subsequently include these points was denied by the lawyer. Finally, the contract did not go through because the Arab business partner felt betrayed.

Something to consider: Companies have their policies and they stick to them. The above case study shows that the sales representative made promises that simply did not conform to company policy. Thus, he put himself and his whole company in a very bad negotiating position. Because the Arab partner, of course, was expecting the sales representative to keep his word and that American companies would only send managers to negotiate who were high enough in the hierarchy to be authorized to not only make the offers, but also to close the deal.

It's extremely important for the Arab business people to sit across from a person "on their level." Being on the same hierarchical level as that of the business counterpart is a show of respect. Don't ever forget the importance of hierarchy when doing business in the Gulf.

This is what international business people say:

If you're not the final decision maker, then, during the negotiations, you need to say, "We're going to prepare the individual points of the contract with you, and I'll give the OK, but everything we agree has to be approved by the management." It is very, very important to say this. Of course, the local businessman will be disappointed, but it needs to be said clearly and precisely! – **Werner Piefer, German businessman. Branch: Safety Technology.**

This is what Arab business people say:

The word is more than a contract in Saudi. And if you don't have the authority to make a final decision you need to say, "Let me get back to you for my approval." Don't say you'll do something and change your mind later. That doesn't work! – **Mohammed Alkhalil, prominent Saudi Arabian businessman, active in diverse fields of business.**

Pitfall 4

Result: A spectacularly unsuccessful joint venture.

What's happening: "Falling in love with the picture" without a fact check. This cannot be the starting point of a long-term business relationship. It certainly leads to an end of the business relationship.

CASE STUDY

I remember a successful businessman from the Gulf, who entered into a partnership with a large, very well-known European food company. The chemistry between the two parties was perfect, right from the word go the Arab partner was enthusiastic about the product. The Europeans were happy to have finally met such a "shining example" of an Arab businessman – a likable and competent personality in the Gulf. He also proved this by inviting his partners to his home and introducing them to distinguished people from the Gulf – a sign of a good network and reputation in his own country. And, other business people from the Gulf, as well, confirmed that he was a very successful businessman. Therefore, both parties trusted each other and began their cooperation in good spirits.

After a year, sales of the product started to drag. And when there was no rise in profits after two years, the business partners met up again. Well, this meeting had a totally different tone than the one two years previously. Each side showered the other side with complaints, phrases like, "Why didn't you do that?" or, "It was actually your job!" Neither of the two parties wanted to invest money in marketing measures, even though both of them were convinced that this was the crucial next step, which could've brought positive change to a hopeless situation. The following year, there was also no increase in turnover. Twelve months later, the international company broke up the relationship with their Arab partners. Both of them were engaged in nasty legal battles, whereby they not only lost money but also their reputation and the respect of the community in the Gulf.

Something to consider: What went wrong here?

Finding 1: The European side had not checked to see what experience the Arab businessman had in the food industry – namely, none. Although he was very successful in other businesses in the Gulf, he was not involved in that sector. And that was why he could not take the necessary strategic steps. This is where the Europeans could have taken action: They should have tested, with different methods, their partner's business competence in the relevant market, right from the start. And they should have run a fact check of their future business partner, before they gave themselves over to the euphoria of a "business marriage."

Finding 2: Obviously, neither of the two parties, the European nor the local, had considered exactly how this product should be placed on the market and that it would demand a large-scale advertising campaign. Furthermore, it was not clear who would bear the financial investment – the local partner or the producer in Europe? Or both? At that time both of them already felt very much "in love with the picture" – the idea of having already found the right business partner. They imagined their own expectations of the partner because they already had the confirmation that he had very good contacts and was well respected in his own community. Consequently, the European side assumed the product would be an immediate success.

This example of an approach, inevitably doomed to lead to the failure of the business partnership, proves unrealistic expectations have hidden pitfalls. From the onset, expectations should be managed in an organized way, making it clear what a realistic outcome would and could be. Now, let's examine how to do this in more detail:

The 5-step program for managing your expectations

Step 1: The decision to deal with your expectations

Come to an agreement with yourself: "I'm ready to look more closely at my inner expectations!" This decision must be an honest one, made from "within" – only then can it work. And only then are the steps you take powerful enough to be effective.

Step 2: Don't generalize about local business people

For this step, let us stick to managing our own thoughts. This is about proactively getting rid of existing prejudgments about people in the Gulf. You know what I'm talking about – basic stereotypes about locals – such as, they are never on time, but all of them are very hospitable and fun to be around.

The list of prejudgments is endless and fertile ground for unfulfilled expectations and the disappointment that goes with it – because maybe an Arab business person might not react in the way you think.

Try this: If "Relentless Judgment" keeps constantly popping up in your thoughts, uninvited, speaking to you from within, determined and knowledgeable, or when a surge of classic negative stereotypes comes over you, then hold still, relax and breathe in and out. Ask yourself:

What's happening to me? Are these truths that I know about my Arab business partner? Or only what I think I know, because it reminds me of other business partners? Are these facts or does my inner "Relentless Judgment" want to talk me into something?

If that's the case, then immediately stop "Relentless Judgment" and say to it, loudly: "Excuse me! It's true that people from the Gulf have their own behavior patterns. But that doesn't mean my Arab business partner is like that. So, dear 'Relentless Judgment,' I'm asking you, politely, to relax! And leave me in peace!" Repeat this sentence again and again. Then you'll calm "Relentless Judgment" and you can begin to devote yourself to more meaningful work: finding out what your Arab business partner is really like.

Remember: "The greatest discovery of any generation is that human beings can alter their lives by altering the attitudes of their minds." This is not a brilliant thought on my part, but something Albert Schweitzer once said. And it's true. You are the director of your own film, your thought process!

Step 3: Don't project your state of mind on your business partner

Imagine the following situation. You, as an international business person, have a great meeting with a potential partner. In parting you agree to contact him when you're ready to present your proposal. You work on it, and the day comes when it's done. Full of positive emotions and good thoughts, you reach for the phone to call your partner. He picks up and says in a strained voice, "OK, I'll get back to you." You say goodbye and are totally disappointed. You ask yourself: Why did my business partner react like that? He was so positive and enthusiastic at the meeting?

Something to consider: You don't know the situation the person at the other end of the line is facing in this particular moment. You might be all set, but is he ready? Maybe he's lost in thought about a message he just received that is distracting him. Or perhaps he's someplace where he can't talk freely, possibly at the "place of sitting" in a *Majlis*, or in the *Diwan*, where he's surrounded by people and can't discuss business. There are many reasons for his reaction. And it doesn't always mean that he's not interested.

Try this: If, all at once, you're gripped by a feeling of profound disappointment, visualize your partner hanging from a cliff, on a rope. In a situation where he needs to be very focused. Smile to yourself, and tell him, very respectfully, "Of course. Thank you. I look forward to hearing from you." Then end the conversation. The Arab business partner's actions, in the next few days, will reveal the true cause of his behavior. (See the chapter on "Communication Culture with the Arab Business Code.")

Step 4: Ask your partner what he expects

In the course of my talks with Arab business people, I have noticed that many expectations were frequently repeated in the same form. In addition, there are many points that reappear in the chapter "Golden Rules" in this book. Here are some examples:

- Importance of long-term goals – both parties should want to "grow old" together.
- Commitment – not giving up, international business people should commit to the partnership even in times of crisis.
- Support of the growth of the Gulf States and of the Arab business partners.

There are also other ways of finding out exactly what your potential local partner expects from you.

Try this: Simply ask your partner how he would describe good cooperation. What he expects. For this, apply communication techniques using the Arab Business Code, where you don't ask direct questions, but gather information and read between the lines. For example: "So, I hear you've had successful business relationships with international partners. What did you like about working with them?"

Step 5: Be prepared for all eventualities

There are many international companies that invest a lot of time and effort into the perfect preparations. Because if you not only have a plan A, but a plan B and C as well, you greatly increase your chances of a successful business venture.

This is what international business people say:

I worked out a price with my Arab business partner, we agreed on it. At the next meeting, the contract was supposed to be signed. Before this meeting, I ran through all the possible scenarios in my head, what I might expect. Also, the possibility that my partner might start the price negotiations again, to try to lower the price. And for that too I was prepared. That's why I had different versions of plan A, plan B and plan C. Plan B was the first price reduction. Plan C was my final price, the price under which I can't go any lower. So, I told my partner, "All right. This is my last offer. If you really agree to this price and sign now, we have a deal." In one such situation, the partner responded right away with, "I agree, that's how we'll do it." So, I pulled the contract (plan C) out of my briefcase and we signed it. – **German businessman. Branch: Automobile Industry.**

Try this: Make a list of everything that might happen. Start with the Arab partner's lateness to the meeting, go to the tricky questions that he could ask. How will you react if your partner, for example, is called out of a meeting? These are things one doesn't usually think of ahead of time. Then you become frustrated and react emotionally, which can be damaging for your business together. Remember: "Frustrated Expectation" really loves for these kinds of situations to take over! In order to manipulate you!

CHAPTER 2

Finding a partner
The search for the ideal business partner begins

Take the time to choose the right partner. It's the most important invest-ment. And then go for it! Then you will succeed. Then it will be like a successful marriage! – **Khalid Almoayed, prominent Bahraini businessman, head of a large family enterprise active in diverse areas.**

Well, you've done your homework and know how to prepare for suc-cessful efforts in the Gulf. You're also aware of the importance of your personal attitude, as well as how to position yourself as a good partner. What's left now is a key question: Who's the right partner for you? What criteria must they meet, what characteristics should they have? This chapters deals with the search for Mr. or Ms. Right.

This is what international business people say:

What I've learned in the last few years: take a good look at the indi-viduals. Don't be blinded. Nor euphoric. Invest the time to study these people closely! – **Michael Gleitsmann, Austrian manager. Branch: Textiles.**

What you need to know: There are many ways of finding the right business partner, from recommendations of the family tribes to visiting "the place of sitting." Many Arab business people have their "place of sitting" in their own home where they receive family members, friends, but also business partners. This ritual of meeting and chatting on a regular basis originates from the past. Back then there was no way of spreading news through television, newspapers or social media. And politics also had to be discussed somewhere. "A place of sitting" was ideal for this. Even today, government leaders use the *Majlis* or the *Diwan* to receive official delegations of a political nature. Equally exciting is an invitation to such "a place of sitting." You must absolutely accept an invitation of this sort!

Now, let's look at what type of person the "right" business partner should be. This needs to be clear before you begin the search. Who exactly are you looking for? What characteristics should they have?

2.1 THE DESIRED BUSINESS PARTNER

This is what Arab business people say:

From the beginning, you need to have a clear concept. What kind of personality are you looking for? And what should this partner's responsibilities be? – **Sheikh Nahayan Mabarak Al-Nahayan, member of the Abu Dhabi ruling family, and a businessman active in diverse areas.**

Knowing exactly what you want is the first important step. From the beginning you need to ask: Do I want a business partner who works full-time, who lives for this business and is active in it? Or is this someone who only sees this venture as an additional source of income, and is not interested in making decisions, someone who wants to stay in the background, someone who doesn't have a say? That needs to be clear from the start. – **German businessman, Branch: Food Industry.**

We knew exactly what we wanted. We wanted a partner who had good contacts, who supported us in the administrative processes and visa applications. Someone who could open doors in the Gulf. What we didn't want was a partner who wanted to take an active part in our business – that much was certain – we wanted to do it ourselves because our experiences have shown that this kind of business constellation can often have extremely negative consequences. It's often the case that business partners, who are part or majority owners of the company, don't understand the specific business areas you are active in. And later, when you're working together, this can be very counterproductive. – **Austrian businessman. Branch: Construction.**

What you need to know: You need to work out for yourself, what kind of business partner you're looking for – that's the crucial first step!

Your specific expectations of the potential partner should be clear. So, you need to come up with a profile.

This leads us to a very helpful technique – creating a profile of your local desired business partner.

Try this: Visualize your perfect business partner, just like you would envision the man or woman of your dreams. So please, don't just answer: "It's simple, he needs to be honest, pay on time." You need to dig deeper. So, here's the question again: What do I expect from my business partner? What should their profile be like? What values should this person have? How should they view the world? Write it all down, in as much detail as possible, from the character traits to the desired professional expertise.

What you'll probably notice, in compiling this list, is that you don't really have an exact idea of how your partner should be. Especially true if your expectations go beyond the surface and deal more intensely with characteristics. Should they be generous, funny? That part is easy. But what about their hobbies, or his education? Can you answer that? Try it and see what happens.

A word of advice: Don't let your work process be manipulated by your "Aggressive Inner Critic" (one of the Seven Emotional Hinderers when doing business in the Gulf – see Appendix) who might be whispering to you, "What nonsense, you'll never find a business partner like that!" This inner attitude is simply counterproductive, and we'll look at this more in more detail in Chapter 5.6. "Praise with the Arab Business Code." In contrast to this mental game, the pros and cons of the ideal partner are by no means absurd but indeed helpful in creating a profile. My long years of studying international business people in the Gulf have convinced me of this, because the most successful entrepreneurs knew exactly the kind of business partners they needed and they were not misled by superficialities, which unfortunately led other business people to fail. Let's examine this problem further.

2.2 FALLING IN LOVE WITH THE PICTURE . . .

It's very seductive, for all of us, to "fall in love" with a superficial picture – in all kinds of human relationship constellations. Particularly, if you are under time pressure and urgently need to find a business partner, or investor, then the temptation to act fast is especially great.

CASE STUDY: *Problem solver instead of partner*

This is what international business people say:

> We picked a very well-known Arab business partner with majority shares in the company. What we didn't realize was that he'd chosen us out of pure necessity because he had a current problem with the water supply for one of his projects and needed help with this. He wasn't at all interested in the further development of our project together. This was something we'd never considered; we were so enthusiastic that we'd finally found a partner. He was a respected businessman and showed us all his big projects in his first meeting. We were impressed, let ourselves be blinded, because all the indicators were basically right. He even organized meetings for us. But we never managed to get a single deal. Today, we know, we hadn't done our homework. We didn't ask any in-depth questions. And we didn't look closely enough at the partner. – **German businessman, active in many areas of business.**

This is what Arab business people say:

> This is what some international companies do not do – they come, have a nice talk and then they decide very quickly with whom they'll cooperate. And then the venture doesn't take off. That's why you have to check your partner very carefully at the beginning! You need to have the right partner – that's my advice. Otherwise you're bound to have problems. – **Issa Alrawahi, well-known Omani businessman. Branch: Oil and Gas Industry.**

What you need to know: This kind of superficiality can go very wrong and mean more trouble and money than it's worth. The Arab businessman touched on this in his statement, and our work with lawyers has confirmed that unsuccessful cooperation can get out of hand, not only due to disagreements, but can also have very painful consequences. If the Arab partner doesn't pull out of the contract, this kind of ill-fated relationship could be dragged through the courts for years and entail high additional costs. That's why you need to wisely consider with whom you're ready to enter into business marriage. And just in case, prepare an exit strategy!

Call to action: Protect yourself in advance from a euphoric "delusion of love" on a superficial level and make the necessary preparations. This begins by playing out all the possible consequences in your head.

Another important tip: What counts is the involvement of the Arab partner – not his name or position!

This is what international business people say:

Today I know, no matter how rich the person's family is, or how good his ties to the royal family are – that has nothing to do with how rich he himself is. And also, not how strong this partner might be in a business joint venture – **German businessman. Branch: Food Industry.**

This is what Arab business people say:

My advice: look for a real local businessman who's actually running his own business. A hard- working man at the top of his industry. I've seen foreigners who partner with locals to open doors for them, to get them access to VIPs and ministers but these locals never did any business. It's also very important that you meet your partners in offices. I don't meet partners in palaces or airports, or in London or Paris. I have to come to their place of business to find out what they're really doing. And whether they are really serious, these guys. – **Dr. Abdulrahman Alzamil, prominent businessman from a big business family of Saudi Arabia, active in diverse fields of business.**

Something to consider: Here we must explicitly note that there are many sheikhs and members of ruling families who are very good at business and very competent and successful businessmen. But it's all about your sense of responsibility – taking active steps and doing a reality check on your potential business partners. Because only after detailed research can you judge if you've found a suitable "better half." Let's go on to consider the best way to proceed.

2.3 REALITY CHECK WITH THE ARAB BUSINESS CODE

It sounds very simple: take a good look at your Arab counterpart – right from the start! That's something you'd do anyway in any kind of relationship, before you enter into a serious commitment or marriage, for example.

This is what Arab business people suggest:

Don't jump at the first one, take a look at all of them. I would ask around among people I know and trust their advice. I'd ask the embassy to give me some information. I'd look at their files, go to their banks. Read about them in newspapers. Everything I can think of. – **Fouad M.T. Alghanim, prominent Kuwaiti businessman, of a large family enterprise active in many business areas.**

As this Arab businessman rightly says, you have to decide to take all possible steps beforehand, to find out even more about your future business partner. Here are two methods you can use for this.

1. Fact check

Of course, for large projects it's customary to do due diligence on the partner's company, with the help of external consultants. But here I'd like to talk about my own personal experiences of how Arab business people select their partners. In my years of talks with them, four parameters they use to check the suitability of business partners have become apparent.

- **Know your partner's business.** Make sure you're dealing with the right people. Check their economic track record and professional competence, their business results, their core competencies.
- **Make sure they have already partnered with others successfully.** Do a background check on them to find out what happened with other partners in the past. Ask around in your communities, talk to other partners directly.
- **Check their experience in your field.** Let them show you they are really able to fulfill your requirements. Read case studies about former similar projects.
- **They have to love their country.** You need to find out by asking them questions like, "What do you think about your country?" and, "Are you proud of your country?" Remember, if they don't care about their country, their country will not care about them.

Call to Action: Have the courage to learn more about your potential partner. Don't be afraid of possible disappointments. They could protect you, up front, from painful consequences. This is, ultimately, the opportunity to really find the right partner. As the saying goes: "Better a horrible end, then unending horror." After all, you want to lead a lasting, successful business relationship. So, have the courage to look deeper and to put the necessary time into it.

A good tool for this is a list of questions – here are some examples:

- Who is the potential partner? What do they specialize in?
- How is their current business performance and what is the goal their company is trying to reach?
- What exactly is their interest in your partnership? Is it only for instant satisfaction?
- How does the service market work in the Gulf state you want to be active in, and how well placed is your future partner in this market?
- How good are their connections in your branch of business? Do they have the corresponding distribution channels and production contacts?
- Have they completed successful projects in your line of business?

Now it's your turn, complete this list here . . .

Conclusion: After you have answered the whole list of questions and your inner voice says, "Yes, this person can really promote me, he knows the right people, he knows how to sell. With him I will win!" – only then, when you are really convinced, can you go for it, sign the agreement or make the deal.

2. Personality check

You can't teach an old dog new tricks and you can't teach a young dog old tricks either! People have their personality, their values. Therefore, you have to keep an eye on your business partner from the start. There are always signs, very small ones, that reveal a lot about their character and the kind of values that are important to them. This you need to know as it will affect your business dynamics in the future a lot. – **Ahmed Hassan Bilal, prominent Qatari businessman. Branch: Real Estate, Hospitality, Media.**

Besides the business compatibility, the chemistry between the active participants also needs to be right. How do you find out what your future business partner's personality is like, the values he holds, if he's more active or reactive? I've asked numerous international companies about the effective procedures and tools they use for this. Here are two of them.

Tool 1: Respectfully asking around in the partner's circles

This is what international business people say:

> We look at these people very closely beforehand. Above all, we talk to other business people at the location, who have already worked with them. Mostly they will only say good things about fellow locals. But it all depends on how they say it. You have to listen carefully. It's a matter of how something is worded. If it's a spontaneous comment like: "He's a good friend, you can trust him!" then this statement is true. You can sense he has had good experiences with the person in question. But if he's trying to talk his way around it, then the opposite is true. And if I get this kind of reaction from several locals then I listen more carefully. Then that's a totally different kind of answer. You get the sense that there have been problems with this person in the past. – **German businessman, active in many sectors.**

What you need to know: The above businessman is talking about how to read between the lines, and to filter out the local's honest answer. More on this in Chapter 5, "Communication Culture with the Arab Business Code." The key point in the above statement is how to check out the partner in a diplomatic way, without embarrassing him in his community or causing him to lose face, and getting a first impression about what's being said about your potential business partner, in the business circles of his own country. This can be vital information in the early stages.

Call to Action: Go to "a place of sitting" like a *Majlis* or the *Diwan* and diplomatically drop questions into your chats with the locals because the personal statements of the future partners cannot have the same informative value as the public image, the view of the community. If several people hesitate to give you answers about your potential partner, then I suggest you pay attention to this and keep researching other options.

Tool 2: Actions should follow words – diplomatically checking if what's been said is true

CASE STUDY: *The test – the pre-license*

This is what international business people say:

> *I needed a trade license. My potential local partner, a very distinguished businessman from Qatar, who was related to the ruling family, said he could procure it for me. This was not something I could rely on, I needed to know for sure. That's why I asked him prior to the signing of the contract, if he could send me the license beforehand, arguing I needed it for an export permit in Germany. He reacted by saying: "No problem! Let me call my secretary. She'll send it to you." And she did. At that moment, it became clear to me: it was done, he really did get the license. –* **German businessman. Branch: Food Industry.**

What you need to know: This businessman had a smart strategy. He didn't let himself be blinded by the famous name or family ties but took matters into his own hands and did a reality check. And the way he did it fulfills all the criteria of successful communication in the Gulf: He cares about his Arab counterpart "not losing face" and he waits patiently for the reply of the local. If the Qatari had said, "Why do you need the license now?" or some other kind of excuse, then the businessman would've known that this man did not have access to it and was therefore the wrong business partner for him.

One more thing: always follow the unwritten rules, never express distrust in the Arab business partner's words or actions. That's an absolute no-go in the Gulf! The resulting loss of respect, trust, and even "loss of face" would certainly hinder the forming of a partnership. The same goes for you. Find out, by diplomatic means, if you will actually get what is being promised to you. There are lots of ways of doing this.

CHAPTER 3

Two innovation strategies
for the Arab Business Code

In the previous chapters we addressed how you can prepare yourself for business success in the Gulf. You heard how important it is to have the right inner attitude, do thorough research, manage your expectations well – and how to choose your ideal partner. Before I convey to you the three golden rules for good business relationships and explain the dos and don'ts in Arab communication, I'd like to introduce two innovation strategies that you can, and should, apply to every situation in the Gulf. Both are based on my years of experience in the Gulf and close observation of Arab business people. Whether you are closing a deal through negotiations or chatting to a sheikh in a *Majlis*, keep these techniques in the back of your mind – they will help you reach your goals.

3.1 THE FITO TECHNIQUE

FITO is short for "From Inside To Outside" and means that your positive inner attitude is, always, a prerequisite for success. Only if you are personally absolutely convinced of your offer or project, and truly want to work together with the Arab partners, will you reach your goals in the Gulf.

In my observations of international business people who have had long-term success in the Gulf, I've noticed the following:

- These business people genuinely like their Arab counterparts and are truly fascinated by the region and the cultural conditions.
- They give their Arab business partners insight into their personalities and are prepared to show emotions.

- These people set boundaries and take up positions at the same time, but always with the clear intention that it "turns out well" for both parties. The general consensus is we want to be successful together – *with* our business partner from the Gulf.
- And, the most important point: all of these business people really mean what they say – their thoughts are sincere and come from their most "inner" core. It is indeed this authenticity that the Arab business people from the Gulf sense and respond to.

That's the FITO technique, which you will keep encountering throughout this book. In diverse case studies, I will provide evidence, again and again, of the usefulness of this technique. Not only international business people, but all people in the Gulf apply this technique. A good example is the reform movements in the Gulf – the social changes that have been implemented have occurred "from the inside out."

This calls to mind my book, *Modern Arab Women*. In it I show how the local women manage, in their own country, to change old views and values from within themselves. First of all, in their immediate families, then, with the help of their own families, they convince their extended families, and ultimately the whole society in the Gulf. The result: today many of these women are respected personalities in their country – successful businesswomen, ministers, filmmakers, and even race car drivers. All of these women have one thing in common: they have, without noticing it, applied the FITO technique because they always operated "from the inside out." And that is why these changes have been lasting and successful.

This is what international business people say:

> Any change that has a good outcome in the Gulf region has to come from the inside. The people will resent change it if it comes from the outside. They need to arrive at their own conclusions. It's part of their tribe, it's part of their cultural history and their tribal identification. – **Dale Karraker, American businessman. Branch: Aerospace, Energy.**

The words of this businessman ring true. When the time came for me to make important decisions in the Gulf, I too realized I was continuously applying the FITO technique. Operating "from the inside out" was effective. First, the families sat down to participate in lengthy discussions, within the "group." There they developed new ways of thinking about society, which were later presented to the heads of family clans.

Three concrete examples illustrate this.

CASE STUDY: *Outstanding debts of local governments were settled*

A Gulf State was in the process of great financial restructuring. There were outstanding debts to international business people. This generated heated debate in the groups. People were very aware of how irresponsible these actions were, how damaging they were to the reputation of the whole country and how much trust had been broken through them. The intense "inner" discussion about starting payments right away was then brought before the governing leader. Of course, with the utmost respect and in the mode of Arab Communication Culture, he was informed of all the arguments discussed within the group and provided a plan of solutions. The leader understood what was at stake. The opinion of the group was important to him. Within a month, the first payments were made.

CASE STUDY: *Quickly changing law – no visas required*

At one time, a Gulf State suddenly introduced visa requirements for a certain international country, calling for particular information that was not customary. This came out of the blue and completely astonished all those involved. The reason for this move was that the Gulf State in question was angered by the visa requirements, and the stricter conditions its citizens faced when travelling to this specific country. Thus, the Gulf State reacted and gave a clear "signal" to express their feeling about this insult. But what actually happened was the people of this Gulf State were embarrassed by this action because it in no way corresponded to the spirit of hospitality so central to their culture. So began the "internal" talks. And the "group" – the families in the Gulf – had heated discussions about this, namely, arguing that this move was simply unacceptable. A month later, the visa requirement was dropped and things went back to the way they were before. Here, too, the power of the group had won over and, "from the inside out," their view prevailed.

And then, a third case study that indeed made the rest of the world sit up and take note. The Saudi Arabian King announced that the driving ban for women in Saudi Arabia was lifted. Here, as well, it is easy to see that the FITO technique played a major role in the King's decision. Years ago, I personally experienced local leaders sitting down to heated discussions on why revoking this driving ban was so important. And here the Saudis, among themselves, in their own families, among their own relatives, but also among friends and acquaintances, convinced each other with strong arguments that there was more to be gained than lost by revoking the driving ban. This constant discussion even led to the country's conservatives viewing the issue from a new angle. I'm not saying that everyone in the country was persuaded but one person was definitely convinced by this FITO technique – the king of Saudi Arabia. He felt "inwardly" strengthened by the group and so he could act "outwardly" in a clear way. Thus, a momentous reform could be implemented.

This is what Arab business people say:

This is our kind of "lobbying" – visiting our open Majlises *around the city where people understand the importance of the development of the business community and the development of the country. To start to talk with big businessmen and ministers on how to develop the country. And then it reaches the big top guys.* – **Bander Alzamil, Saudi Arabian businessman of a large, global family enterprise, active in diverse areas.**

3.2 THE GAS-SHIFT-BRAKE TECHNIQUE

During my stays in the Gulf I saw that successful business people, in all their actions – be they verbal or non-verbal – always applied one technique to maintain a balance. Consequently, they avoided appearing pushy but still managed to actively pursue their goals. This made me curious! So, I analyzed this technique in detail and gave it a name: The "Gas-Shift-Brake" technique. Why? Because it reminds me of driving a car. It's best demonstrated through a case study.

CASE STUDY: *The perfect business call*

When you direct the first words at your Arab business partner on the phone, then you're stepping "on the gas." You're providing input, spreading positive energy, setting a good mood. For example: "Good afternoon, this is Judith from Vienna, how are you?" Your tone is friendly, pleasant. After all, the person taking the call should be happy to hear your voice. Once you've said a few sentences, listen to your counterpart carefully. What is their response? How does this person sound? Are they under stress? Are you interrupting something? On the basis of this reaction and the actual acoustic statements, try to sense how they are feeling. If the person on the other line is not asking any questions, then you need to shift gears. Ask in a gracious manner: "Am I disturbing you? Are you in a meeting? Shall I call you a little bit later?" Maybe the local business person is in a situation where they can't speak freely but does not want to be rude and put you off – you know, the politeness of the Arab world. To honor their wishes, you should apply this technique. By shifting down a level, you are offering them another option and helping to maintain their free space. Don't force them by applying pressure to continue the conversation. That would be counterproductive.

Maybe the Arab business person will say: "No problem, how are you?" This will signal that you can continue talking. So, shift to a higher gear. And then step on the gas. Ask personal questions, about how the family is doing and so on. Now you're on the road and building up the positive atmosphere. Meanwhile, always listen actively to the party on the other line – what is this man or woman saying? How does their voice sound? Are they asking questions? Do they still seem interested and involved in the conversation? Or do they seem bored? If so, then give it more gas!

It could also be that the person you're talking to, though interested in what you're saying, is still distracted by something. Maybe someone has just walked into his room and addressed him. In the Arab world it's very common to talk to several people at the same time. In such a case, follow it up with questions and shift down a gear if you need to.

By shifting between the individual gears, going slower or faster, you can hear what resonates with your Arab counterpart. What exactly did he understand? And here the Gas-Shift-Brake technique is very useful! With this approach you don't become pushy – something people in the Gulf absolutely dislike. With this technique, you wrap your key message in a mixture of praise and friendliness. That's how you create a good mood. But you also convey respect and still stay focused on your goal.

The following case study of an international company shows how the Gas-Shift-Brake technique is applied effectively in business cooperation to successfully close intense or prolonged negotiations.

CASE STUDY: *With cigarette breaks toward the signing of the contract*

This is what international business people say:

One business negotiation with Arab partners lasted for hours. The Arab businessmen were under time pressure and had to decide quickly, as the contract was expected at the ministry by 2 pm for signing. With this knowledge in mind, I began, at the start of the meeting, to go into detail about the advantages that justified our price. (Note: here the businessman steps on the gas and shifts to a higher gear). *The partners, of course, could not accept this price and tried again to negotiate a cost reduction. Then I got up and said: "Mr. Ahmed, we need a cigarette. We can't go on like this."* (Note: here, the businessman is shifting down to a lower gear and he'll tap the brake to slowly bring it to a stop.) *Our counterparts were beginning to sweat, because the ministry was about to close. I said: "I'm very sorry, but there's no point to this. I just can't do this price. We've been discussing it for four hours. I need a break and a cigarette."* (Note: here, "by pressuring" again, the businessman gradually shifts to a higher gear.) *I was already at the door* (Note: the businessman is "applying maximum pressure" – is in the highest gear at this point) *when the Arab negotiation partner said to me, "Please sit down – we'll sign the contract now!"* – **German businessman. Branch: Construction.**

CASE STUDY: *Defining the final price – seven hours and fifteen coffee breaks*

This is what international business people say:

I was in negotiations that lasted seven hours. With fifteen coffee breaks. At first, we spoke privately (Note: here, you leave the motor running, put it into first gear and give it a little gas), *then we were negotiating on a business level* (Note: then you stay in the same gear for a while – you're on the road, so to speak).

After some time, you switch to small talk and personal topics (Note: that is the downshift). *And that's how the whole conversation continued – gas, shift, brake – switching between personal topics and price negotiations. It lasted for hours. But at some point, we reached a final price.* – **Martina Schwarz, Austrian business-woman. Branch: IT Industry.**

What you need to know: Especially in the Arab Communication Culture, you can have highly successful talks with the Gas-Shift-Brake technique. It makes it easier for you to avoid placing too much pressure on your Arab counterpart and maintaining a balance. Above all, it's necessary to step on the brakes, every once in a while, because Arab decision makers will not be convinced by force or pressure.

This is what international business people say:

Trying to force an Arab businessman to make a decision just won't work. No matter how much you want the negotiations to come to an end, or to close the deal. If you push harder, it won't get you anywhere. The opposite is actually successful: go to the customer without trying to push something on him. Don't give the impression he has to do this right away. Don't tell him when it's the right time for this. That won't work. Just be relaxed and carry on a well-balanced conversation. – **Austrian businessman. Branch: Automobile Industry.**

The Gas-Shift-Brake technique can also teach you to say "No" gracefully. Here are a few case studies of this.

CASE STUDY: *Set boundaries – when the Arab counterpart appears disrespectful and uninterested*

This is what international business people say:

I had a meeting with a young Arab businessman. He was almost an hour late – these things can happen. But after we had introduced ourselves and I had begun my presentation, he leaned back in his chair and started to fiddle with his mobile phone. He kept casting bored looks at me and his phone. Finally, he asked me with a voice drained of energy: "Do you have a brochure?" I said no. He asked again: "You don't have a brochure?" And this question was even more apathetic. It was really disgusting. As if he had said to me: "So why am I here with you?" In that moment there was only one thing left to do – I stood up and said politely, and with the utmost respect: "Thank you for your time! If you ever want to have a serious talk, let me know. You can call me then." A few weeks later, he really did call for an appointment, where he offered me the job of con-structing a factory. We actually built the factory together. But what we never mentioned, in any of the following meetings, was our first conversation. Not a single word about it. – **German businessman. Branch: Food Industry.**

Let me deal with this example in more detail, because this behavior isn't something I'd usually recommend for every type of business rela-tionship. Although the way the German businessman conducted him-self here was appropriate because he'd done a solid analysis of strengths and weaknesses – he knew beforehand that he had a strong negotiating position and was very aware of his Arab counterpart's position.

Without prior knowledge of the Arab Business Code, the interna-tional businessman would not have dared to speak out with such a clear "No." Thus, pull the handbrake. This businessman was appar-ently fully aware of the consequences – namely, that it might end the business relationship because some Arab business people will not put up with this kind of behavior. But this business situation was simply different.

Let's see exactly what happened: The businessman is, so to speak, on the road, but quickly notices that his Arab partner is not display-ing any interest. It makes no sense to step on the gas in this situation, that's why he has to use the emergency brakes, and say: "Get back to me when you're interested." We know the rest of the story. The partner gets in touch and the businessman starts "driving" again, using the Gas-Shift-Brake technique.

The Gas-Shift-Brake technique can even support you in giving your honest opinion to your Arab partner and still get the deal. Here's a case study on this.

CASE STUDY: *I could switch off your main operation in just five minutes! How can you say that?*

This is what international business people say:

> *Through a joint venture in the Arab Gulf I got a glimpse into a security operation, which could normally only be accessed with top VIP security passes. It was in a terrible state. After a third of the tour had passed, I got the chance to present our company's work to the number three person of this organization. High ranking generals were also there.*
>
> *After my short presentation, I was asked for my opinion on their security system. At first, I noted many positive aspects, but then also mentioned a few critical points that needed to be dealt with. During my criticism all the generals smiled in a polite and friendly way. I sensed that my message was not getting through to them, simply because they didn't want to hear bad news and have to deal with it. But I remained persistent – because my goal was to be taken seriously. Otherwise, the whole tour would've been in vain. That's why I fixed my eyes on one of the generals. He reacted with a look: "What´s wrong?" So, I responded by saying: "I'm wondering how to make you aware in a polite way about what's going on in your organization. Where you stand when it comes to safety and fire-hazard standards." I carried on: "Let me just put it like this: if I were an intelligence organization, I could switch off your main operation in just five minutes." That hit home – suddenly the decision maker looked at me seriously and asked: "How can you say that?" I outlined it for him precisely; what I could do with the simplest means to paralyze the base in ten minutes. After this conversation I was commissioned to work for them, and we cooperated very well together.* – **Austrian businessman. Branch: Special Vehicles.**

In this case study, we can see the Gas-Shift-Brake technique being applied in a combination of verbal and nonverbal communication. This is how it works: when the businessman starts to speak his praise and criticism, he begins to shift gears. Then he manages to keep the conversation from getting too emotional, because in a higher gear he might lose control. When he's on the road in the highest gear, he looks the general straight in the face. He adds eye contact as a nonverbal means of communication, as a way of stepping on the gas and waits for the reaction of the general, which is immediate. That's why the businessman stays in this gear. And so, the whole conversation continues, operating on the Gas-Shift-Brake principle.

What you need to know: Watch out when using the Gas-Shift-Brake technique. Accelerating too much and racing through the negotiations is counterproductive. The following example, told by an Arab businessman, illustrates what can happen when you leave out the Shift-Brake part of the technique.

CASE STUDY: *Too much pressure*

This is what Arab business people say:

> I had a meeting with a consulting firm working in the electricity sector. They wanted to enter the Gulf market with a new airport project. They were being pressured to make deals. They tried with us for two weeks – ringing every day. Obviously, they were very serious in their attempts to get some projects running. They had a strong commitment – that was great. But it was a new area of business for me so, I needed more time to understand the risks. But they rang me every day and so I finally put the deal on ice. – **Businessman from the United Arab Emirates, active in diverse areas.**

What you need to know: Arab business people, too, need time to access the risks and come to a decision. And I really understand, it's very hard to be patient. But this is the most important factor for success in the Gulf and the Gas-Shift-Brake technique offers enormous support in helping you manage your patience.

Take Action: Train your patience with the help of the Gas-Shift-Brake technique. One exercise is: Imagine a meeting with an Arab businessman. He says he'll call you next week – for sure! However, you don't hear anything from him the following week. Then you call, but he doesn't pick up. His office also doesn't put you through to him, since he's constantly in meetings. What should you do? Think of the Gas-Shift-Brake technique.

- With two calls you have already stepped on the gas.
- Now the time has come to hit the brakes. Visualize yourself putting your foot firmly on the brake pedal.
- Once the car has come to a stop, calmly get out and let it sit parked for a week.
- If the partner has still not contacted you, then try again. Open the car door, start the engine and shift into first gear – call him again.
- If he does pick up or call back, always make sure you apply the Gas-Shift-Brake technique in your telephone conversation. Then you'll be successful.

CHAPTER 4

Three golden rules
of the Arab Business Code

4.1 GOLDEN RULE NO. 1: CHEMISTRY

This is what Arab business people say:

> *Look, chemistry is a very, very important issue. Very important! If we don't "click," I will not give you even one dirham. Because why should I go through all that effort with a person I do not like.* – **Businessman from the United Arab Emirates. Branch: Food, Oil and Gas Industry.**

Without chemistry no business relationship will flourish in the Arab Gulf!

What you need to know about the Arab Gulf: Interpersonal relationships are crucial here – especially in business. Who their counterpart is means a lot. Particularly, how they feel toward this person at that particular moment, the "chemistry" between them.

CASE STUDY: *Creating comfort levels to get the foot in the door – the camel talk*

Let's take the example of an American company who wanted to do business in the United Arab Emirates (UAE). For this the company needed a special license, which was not easy to get – they had been trying for a year but weren't getting anywhere. The US partners were in a stressful situation and wanted to finally get the ball rolling. At last, the manager succeeded in making an appointment with a key Arab businessman. Only fifteen minutes were set aside for this talk. A team of two men from the American party were to attend the meeting, one of them was always just "flying through" from their headquarters in the US to their office in UAE, never staying for more than two or three days a month. He did not know the country and its citizens. The other had lived in the Emirates for over three years and had previously worked in another company in the UAE, so he was very familiar with their business practices and customs. He had also developed a great personal passion for the land and its people.

Arriving to the appointment on time, they exchanged only a few words about the matter of acquiring a license with the help of the Arab businessman. The local and the American living in the UAE fell into casual conversation. The two men talked about the country and its people; they went back and forth between topics of camels, camel racing and even how to breed camels. Both of them got very engaged in the conversation, jumping from subject to subject, without once mentioning the license. The other American colleague was getting more and more anxious – because he knew the Arab businessman's time was limited. They only had fifteen minutes. And now there were only ten minutes left. How was this going to happen? When were they finally going to talk about the license?

And then it happened – the local businessman looked at his watch and said, "I'm terribly sorry, but I'm so busy today. I have another appointment now." The Americans were shocked. They thought, "Oh my god, we lost our opportunity!" But the Arab businessman grabbed a pen and wrote a few things down on a scrap of paper. Then he said, "Look, here is what we'll do. If you do 1, 2, and 3 for me, I'll do A, B, and C for you. And then we can sign the contract." He stood up, said his goodbyes to everybody politely, spending a few more seconds with the American he had conversed with for such a long time. He smiled at him brightly and said, "It was really nice getting to know you!" Then he left the room. The Americans just stood there paralyzed. They couldn't understand what had just happened. For over a year they had been trying, by all means, to get this license. And now, without even discussing the license, but instead talking about camels, the country and its culture, they had managed to get the "go ahead" – finally securing the license and closing the deal. How could that be?

The answer is simple. At this first meeting the Arab businessman wanted to get a sense of the Americans. He "tested the grounds" to see if these people felt pleasant to him. If he had not found them to his liking, he would not have done business with them. It's that simple.

A good feeling is always top of mind – even in business meetings!

This is what international business people say:

I was told that 95 per cent of international partnerships break down or never get off the ground because of faulty chemistry. They never did anything or bought anything. They never created anything. They just spent a lot of money, but nothing happened. The most important part of our success in the Arabian Gulf is chemistry. – **Robert Hofmann, American businessman. Branch: Real Estate.**

There are many stories. For example, I won a contract and, sometime later, I was standing in line at the airport when somebody tapped me on the shoulder. I turned around and there was one of these important guys I had met at our presentation. He smiled at me and I was certain that he had something to do with us winning this contract, that he had a huge influence in this decision – and that he had convinced the other Saudi decision makers that he needed our company at that time – all that because of the chemistry. – **Gary Newman, American manager. Branch: Aerospace**.

This is what Arab business people say:

Before I develop a business relationship with someone, I want to build a personal relationship, to have the confidence in his reliability, commitment and trustworthiness. The personal relationship is equally important as the business relationship itself. The chemistry has to work! – **Dr. Mohammed Al-Barwani, prominent Omani businessman of a large business family active in diverse sectors.**

People say about us, we – the young generation – are a digital generation and that we only like to communicate through social media or the internet, that we do not need personal contact that much. But it doesn't work like that. Face-to-face communication is always the most important thing – also for the young generation. It won't work only by email or digitally. You need to get a feel for the person – the chemistry between two business people must be right. That's important! – **Mishal A. Al Hokair, businessman from a well-known Saudi Arabian business family, active in diverse fields of business.**

Even if I could pay less, how can you deal with somebody you do not feel comfortable with? I had four or five companies who came to me. But I made a deal with the company I felt good with. – **Salah H. Sobghan, well-known Saudi Arabian businessman. Branch: Food Industry.**

The Arab Business Code (ABC): Arab business people need to feel comfortable in a conversation. So, if the chemistry doesn't work from the beginning, how does one build good chemistry with Arab Gulf business partners? Let us focus on this now – here are two of my findings.

Key Code 1: the sixth sense in the Arab Gulf

Be careful what you think! People from the Gulf are mind readers! In every conversation, the locals listen deeply to their inner voice – the so-called sixth sense, or intuition. It is predominately this sixth sense that lets them know if they should do business with someone. This survival instinct helps Arab business people make decisions and provides clarity about the individuals they work with. That's why it's so important to understand their survival instinct.

CASE STUDY: *Even a nonverbal patronizing attitude creates exit scenarios for locals*

I once experienced a meeting between a western businessman and a businessman from Abu Dhabi. They sat opposite each other. Even though the western businessman never directly said, "You will never get this off the ground without us," he still presented his proposal in a very arrogant tone. Somehow you got the impression the western man was patronizing the local. The Arab man listened to this for fifteen minutes – very patiently. And then he told the western man, very graciously and with the greatest respect, "Unfortunately, I have to leave for my next appointment. But it's not a problem, my assistant (a Jordanian) will continue the meeting with you." He got up and said goodbye, "It was a pleasure meeting you. Thank you for taking the time to come here." The western man was left with the assistant who was not in the position to make any decisions, because the person with all the real power had already walked away. From then on, he could not be reached by the western man, not by phone or email. Not even his assistant, who continued to converse politely with the Westerner, could help him gain access. From that moment on, the Arab man was simply extremely busy and not available anymore to the European.

The classic exit scenario with the Arab Business Code (ABC)

What you need to know: When Arab men or women feel "mocked," they withdraw. I term this kind of retreat a "classic exit scenario with the Arab Business Code," whereby Arab business people, in a charming and very well-mannered way, step out of the game, without attracting attention, very diplomatically. They are world masters at that. Sometimes, you only notice they have disappeared when it's already too late, since it all takes place on a nonverbal level. They have a very refined perception mechanism, sensors that seem to enable them to read the thoughts of others.

The Arab Business Code (ABC): People from the Gulf region will not tolerate being lectured to by others. When locals perceive "vibes" that lead them to believe they are being used they react with great sensibility – especially when they feel people are out to get their money; the "international suitcase manager" comes to mind. Have you ever heard of him?

The "international suitcase manager"

The locals like to call businessmen who do not invest a minute more in talks than is absolutely necessary, "suitcase managers." They come to the Gulf for a meeting and the next morning they are back on the first plane home. Consequently, they only travel with a single suitcase and would like nothing more, upon departing the Arab Gulf, than to have that suitcase filled with cash – preferably in big bills; an advance payment from their Arab business partners. Their most faithful companion is "Insatiable Greed" one of the characters of the "Emotional Hinderers in the Gulf." (Also see: Appendix, "More on the Seven Emotional Hinderers when doing business in the Arab Gulf and page directory of the characters.")

"Suitcase managers" do not want to invest one moment longer than necessary in talks with their Arab counterparts. When people from the Gulf deal with these "suitcase managers," they disappear as quickly as possible. They are very sensitive to these types of people. They simply don't like greedy managers. And, they notice when their visitors are not interested in them or their ways of life.

This is what international business people say:

A horse can feel if you do not like it, it's their survival instinct – just like the people from the Arab Gulf can sense the vibe you send off. – **Dean Lavy, American who has been training racehorses, for years, for the heads of Gulf States, selling these horses on the international market for his clients.**

This is what Arab business people say:

We call it the "gut feeling" – your stomach telling you, "This is not safe." And even if all documentation, assumptions and estimates look fine and everybody says it's good – if you are not comfortable don't do it! A lot of times your instinct tells you what is right. It can also work the other way around – it may feel good. Then take a closer look! – **Dr. Mohammed Al-Barwani, prominent Omani businessman of a large business family active in diverse sectors.**

We can read their minds, even if they're talking about something else. They assume we don't know what we are talking about. But believe me, we understand (smiles). And some of them try to be clever, and that's the problem! – **Businessman from Bahrain, who is active in diverse business fields.**

Don't underestimate your Arab business associates! They can sense unspoken things incredibly well. The older generation especially, has highly sensitized antennae – that generation is even more attuned to vibes given off by the people they meet. The reason for this can be traced to when Bedouins and nomads lived in the desert. They fought to stay alive – this built up strong intuition.

The natives of the Gulf speak to me of the "sixth sense" – what the Saudis call *firasah*. It was a highly pronounced sense in desert inhabitants in the past. They perfected the technique of reading traces in the sand. They could tell right away if a man or a woman had crossed the desert. Was the person thin or heavy set? This was quickly discerned by Arab trackers from the depth of the indentations in the sand. They relied on their own senses.

Even in today's world, Arab business people from the Gulf strongly rely on their own perception. This is combined with the body language of the person they meet, their gestures and facial expressions and how it all fits together with what the business person is actually saying. These small pieces of the mosaic of perception merge to form a complete picture of the counterpart. It is a first insight into the inner attitude of the person they intend to do business with. That's why international business people have great trouble hiding behind their learned mode of behavior in negotiations with Arab business people.

For, no matter how talented an actor you are, in the long run it's hard to keep up a façade. At some point the "act" will be exposed. Which brings me to my second finding.

Key Code 2: communicate authentically from the inside out!

You need to have genuine, positive feelings toward people in the Arabian Gulf – from the inside out, only then will it work long term. – **Dean Lavy, American who has been training horses for Gulf State leaders for many years, selling these horses on the international market for his clients.**

It's a fact: what's happening inside you will show itself at some point!

CASE STUDY: *Inner resistance will erupt*

This is what international business people say:

I remember a business meeting between an international and an Arab businessman. The local was talking about something the other businessman seemed to have total inner resistance to, because he began to roll his eyes and shrug his shoulders. This all happened involuntarily and was not in sync with the westerner's nodding in approval to the statements of his counterpart, trying to appear as if he fully agreed with him. But his gestures gave him away – they did not correspond to his words. It was a very unpleasant business atmosphere. Very counterproductive! – **Jean-Pierre Simon, Swiss manager. Branch: Hotel Industry.**

What you need to know: Business people who are not authentic throw locals from the Gulf off balance. A thoroughly negative inner attitude toward your Arab business associate can fracture business ties. Especially in stressful situations, we find it hard to hide our true thoughts. Or if we feel unfairly treated, or things don't go how we'd like them to. Then we might feel a slight shaking, notice ourselves grow warm, have a lump in our throats. Those are the first signals – you can be sure the "Incensed Anger Rascal" has just arrived and is beginning to cheer us on, to finally speak our mind to our Arab counterparts. The body is being mobilized, like the process of a volcano shortly before it erupts. Something like this can be reflected in an uncontrolled facial expression, accompanied by a wrong choice of words. One word leads to the next, and suddenly you're in the middle of it all, the "Incensed Anger Rascal" has triumphed.

I am sure you are familiar with this. You find yourself in a position you never wanted to be in, especially if you are trying to sell your Arab counterpart something.

The worst part of it is you also lose respect for the person you are doing business with! This can have disastrous consequences, especially since respect means so much in the Arab Gulf and has to be reflected in all encounters with Arab business associates.

Call to action: You have to keep your thoughts regarding your Arab business associate positive! As a first step try to admit to yourself any aggression you might have toward the locals.

This is what international business people say:

> *Especially if you are particularly emotional, it can be hard to keep it hidden. At some point it will break out. That is why you need a positive inner attitude toward locals.* – **Jean-Pierre Simon, Swiss manager. Branch: Hotel Industry.**

So, how do I, as an international business person, develop a positive attitude toward my Arab counterparts? Is it something you can build up? The good news first: you can train yourself to have a positive attitude toward people from the Gulf, without giving up any of your values or identity. (See the so-called FITO Technique.) I will keep coming back to this technique in the following chapter, because it is so useful in communicating with local business people.

4.2 GOLDEN RULE NO. 2: FAMILY

In this society everything functions through family ties, the strong family collective. – **Werner Piefer, German businessman. Branch: Safety Technology.**

What you need to be aware of in the Gulf is, in this part of the world the family plays a major role; it is extremely important to people in the Gulf. Let me demonstrate this with a case study on one of my first meetings with a businessman in Abu Dhabi. And I can already tell you, I was in for a surprise! But see for yourself.

CASE STUDY: *The first business meeting – how's your father?*

I was sitting across from an Arab businessman. After we had exchanged general greetings and pleasantries, I was suddenly asked, "How's your father?" I was shocked, but also surprised, and wondered, "How could this man know my father? After all, I'd just met him for the first time." Was I missing something?

What you need to know: People from the Gulf States always ask you about your family – especially about your father and your mother – and it really is an honest question, also among themselves. The family is always at the forefront of every conversation. So, let us analyze the opportunities but also stumbling blocks the family creates in interactions with Arab business people.

Key Code 1: The Power of the word "family"

Option no. 1: "family" as a door opener to business in the Gulf

CASE STUDY: *Positive reinforcement for arranging a follow up meeting*

An international businessman had, in addition to his business cooperation with an Arab business partner, built up a good relationship on a personal level with the local. He took regular drives through the desert with him. They philosophized together over Arabian coffee and hummus, about family matters, hobbies, and life in general. Slowly, a friendship grew between these two men. The Arab businessman even invited him to his wedding.

A few months later, the international businessman met with another local businessman and presented a project to him, suggesting a share in the financing. On parting, the Arab businessman said to the international businessman, "OK, I'll get back to you!" The conversation unsettled him – he didn't have a good feeling because the local hadn't inquired much about the project. But that same evening he got the call; the Arab businessman was asking to schedule a follow up meeting. And, at the end of the phone conversation, the local even said to him, "Looking forward to seeing you again! I'm very interested in working with you." What had happened? The international businessman was confused – the Arab businessman had not really appeared interested during their talk.

What you need to know: There's a specific reason this Arab businessman called the international businessman that same evening. After the two men had said their goodbyes, the Arab businessman got down to the real work. I'm convinced he called all his friends and acquaintances and asked around about his visitor – the international businessman. "Have you ever heard of this man?" Some said "No." But, at some point he had his friend Abdullah on the line, and he told him, "Sure, I know him. He was at my cousin's wedding. A very nice guy. And your uncle Ahmed has worked with him as well."

The two Arab businessmen, most certainly, then went on to chat about the family and other things. After the Arab businessman got off the phone, he was convinced: doing business with this international person was a very viable and interesting option – something to look into much deeper. And, right away, he dialed the number of the businessman to arrange the next meeting.

This is what Arab business people say:

> *When you go through family members and friends, you'll get trust. It's the Arab culture – you come from Ahmed and I trust Ahmed, so I trust you. This is enough. It's is the first opening for business.* – **Faisal Almahroos, well-known businessman from Bahrain. Branch: Oil and Gas Industry.**

The Arab Business Code (ABC): Any choice of words with the Key Code "family" in it, activates a kind of reflex in people from the Gulf region. And this reflex is based on the first trust of Bedouin tribes from the past where inclusion into the family clan ensured survival in the desert. Today, this reflex is still deeply rooted in people in the Gulf, no matter how business oriented and tough they are.

Option no. 2: Key Code of "family" to improve the negotiating position

CASE STUDY: Ace in the pack – "family business"

This is what international business people say:

When I'm sitting down to talks with an Arab business family, and get to a critical point in the negotiations, then I casually mention that I'm also part of a family business, and that this company has existed for over 26 years, with my dad as the "top boss." And imme-diately you can tell that the climate of discussion at the table has improved, as well as my negotiating position! – **Martina Schwarz, Austrian businesswoman. Branch: IT Industry.**

What's evident here: The business woman is consciously playing her ace while negotiating with the Arab business partners. She's doing this skillfully, because she applies the expression of "family" once clearly – and then a second time – packing it in a smaller phrase, adding, "My dad, the top boss." In this way she never risks overusing the Key Code "family" and thereby losing leverage. Because one thing you must never do – never use the expression of "family" in a negative context. This would not only unsettle the business partners, it could even insult them. Let's see where you might stumble in applying the expression of "family."

Stumbling block: negative use of the Key Code "family." Result: distrust and insult.

CASE STUDY: Complaining about neighboring Gulf States to locals is counterproductive

I remember a conversation with an international businessman who had a business partner from Dubai. I had brought the two of them together. When they met for the first time they got along well.

It appeared they had good chemistry and at the end of the meeting, they started talking about private matters. At the time, there was a financial problem in the Gulf and some Arab companies were not paying their international contractors. A big Arab business family from a neighboring Gulf State was especially known for this. Since the international businessman had established trust with his counterpart, he began to speak honestly about the abovementioned family. He insisted that no one should, by any means, do business with this family, it would damage their reputation. The businessman grew more and more emotional as he related this. And at some point, he even said things like, "They're not to be trusted! Every one of them – all liars! It's terrible!" In the meantime, he emphasized – and he looked the man from Dubai straight in the eye. Then he said how different the families in the Emirates are. And that this here is an exception, rather than the rule. The Dubai businessman listened to this very calmly and attentively, without saying a word. The two men said their goodbyes and scheduled another meeting. What the international businessman did not know was that the sister of his potential Arab client was married to someone in the family he had badmouthed, and so, by association, he had also badmouthed this man's family. Furthermore, the local himself had business dealings with a branch of that family – and very successful ones, in fact, because this branch of the family also paid their contractors.

What you need to know: Especially during the financial crisis and the political changes in the Gulf, I noticed some international business people liked to complain, to every Gulf State member they were having business talks or collaborating with, about neighboring Gulf States who happened to have a bad image at the time. And here, no one made the distinction of who's who. This didn't seem to matter, along the lines of, "One Gulf State is just like another." Generalizations such as, "They're all the same! One and the same family!" (Note: "Relentless Judgment" starts manipulating here – see more in the Appendix on the Emotional Hinderers). There was no distinguishing between different branches, even though it was well known that many of them acted completely independently of each other businesswise. And that the branches had different attitudes about values regarding business cooperation, such as paying as agreed.

It would appear, too, that some companies use "complaining to one Gulf State about another" as a way of making a "tribute." Because by saying, "You are different from them" it's obvious the business partner they are talking to at that moment is the better one, not just as a person, but as part of a nation. These kinds of statements, naturally, always feel good and boost confidence, of the Arab counterpart as well. And basically, a praise culture is well received in the Arab world. But not with the technique of "badmouthing the other," for many reasons. So, let's take a closer look at these.

First: The way you talk with a person about their neighboring countries will show your counterpart in which way you could talk about him one day. He'll judge these kinds of statements in a correspondingly critical way, and wonder, "Could this person be a loyal business partner; someone to stand by me in difficult situations?"

Second: As you have just heard in the previous case study, when you criticize a family that the person you are talking to might already be working with, it means that you are, by extension, also criticizing him, judging him to be a bad businessman, because he made the wrong decision of doing business with a partner who has a bad reputation. That reflects on him and gives him a bad image. So, you have just insulted the person across the table from you.

Third: We've already mentioned this – you will never know how people are connected through marriage or blood. The Arab in our case study was, by the marriage of his sister, also a part of the family clan the foreign businessman was criticizing. Hence, the Arab businessman felt "attacked" and "badmouthed," because he's also a part of this family and belongs to the extended family.

Finally: All one can hope for is that you as an entrepreneur will not, one day, need, in a business sense, the family you have badmouthed. Never forget, Arab people are very communicative and talk a lot among themselves – one day they might even talk about you.

This is what international business people say:

That's what I've learned here in the Gulf – never say anything impolite about some other families. Because it's a small community here. You never know who you may insult by saying this. You never know exactly who's who. And you don't understand what they're representing and who they're related to or work with or are friends with. In the US it's clear when you meet the Rockefellers or Kennedys, but here you just don't know. You need to be very careful! – **Robert Hofmann, American businessman. Branch: Real Estate.**

Call to action: Be reserved when it comes to negative statements about other Gulf States, no matter how much you feel like venting, even if it's on the tip of your tongue! Even if you feel you're justified, and this family has owed you, for a long time, big payments. There are more effective ways to communicate this, in a targeted way, to other business people. And then to ultimately get your money. But this "outright badmouthing of the other" is certainly not a recommended technique. I strongly suggest you refrain from doing this because the network of interconnections of individual family members is enormous, even if they do not always agree with the neighboring country's way of doing things.

I remember when a Gulf State got into financial trouble and one of their "brothers," a related Gulf State, dug into its own state pockets to support them with a round figure of $30 billion. This was not publicly communicated, but done "behind the scenes" and was obvious to everyone in the Gulf. A clear message – and there are many similar examples in the Gulf. In the end, the family always sticks together. That goes for the whole Gulf region.

Try this: Be prepared. Do your research and find out who your business partner is related to and what clan he belongs to. Work out these details and recognize the "Who's Who Arab Business Code" – which families have close ties to other families. Possessing this background information will open up a large array of possibilities. For example, how to identify the real Arab decision maker and, thereby, speed up eventual payment claims. Or how to ensure your concern reaches someone close to this decision maker.

Key Code 2: The entire Arab Gulf is "one great big family"

This is what Arab business people say:

I don't know how it is worldwide, but here everybody knows everybody – everywhere you have a friend, a relative, or somebody who knows somebody. The Arab Gulf is like a private club. – **Sameera Jassim Fakhri, prominent businesswoman from Qatar. Branch: Fashion.**

In the Gulf States everyone does know everyone.

You need to be aware of the dimensions we are talking about when we refer to the size of one such Arab family clan. When it comes to the big tribes, it can include around 20,000 people, the medium sized ones are made up of about 5,000 and the smaller ones could have 350 people. This number exceeds the number of inhabitants of some village communities.

The reason for this huge size is because many clans in the Gulf are connected through marriage – Emiratis with Qataris, or with Saudis, all the way to Kuwaitis with Bahrainis or Omanis. This will be especially apparent when you travel around the Gulf and keep hearing the same family names over and over again.

What makes it even more fascinating is that every person in the Gulf States, in some way, has some kind of contact with every other person in the Gulf States. Even if they are not related, they can still reach out to someone who knows this person from the Gulf. For example, the brother of a friend or the cousin of a sister, or maybe the uncle or aunt of an acquaintance, who has personal access. Everything always comes full circle in the Gulf.

Let's take a look at where the opportunities for international business people are in this "club." I have called it the "Arab Business Club."

Arab Business Club

This kind of club somehow reminds me of the world of Formula 1 racing, which I got to know while I worked as a journalist. The individual F1 teams were comparable to the six Gulf States. In no time at all, you could run into financially strong investors and business people. In this Arab Business Club, too, very rapidly, in a pleasant atmosphere, you could meet the most investment happy Arab business people; the Arab business world is an elaborately tight knit network, where all the top players know each other.

So, the question is, how can an international business person become a member of this elite club? It's not officially registered anywhere. Let's take a closer look at it. There are many different ways of joining this club. Here are some examples.

The classic way to "join" the Arab business club and become initiated into its codes

Let's start with the "classic" approach, demonstrated by the following case studies.

CASE STUDY: *Admission ticket on the flight from Doha to Bahrain*

I remember a meeting with an Arab businessman in his office in Doha. In the course of our conversation, I briefly mentioned that I was going to visit the Gulf State of Bahrain the next day. My remark caused the man from Doha to laugh heartily: "Well, then you must visit the husband of my wife's sister! And send him my greetings! He's sure to be happy to see you." So, that's exactly what I did – I met this man. And it turned out this contact was one of the most powerful businessmen in Bahrain. We had a very good conversation and during the meeting the Bahraini offered to introduce me to other Bahraini business people.

CASE STUDY: *Admission ticket to the head of a government agency from brother to brother*

This is what international business people say:

I had a contact who was the head of a municipal agency in Saudi Arabia. While I was sitting across from him and talking, I told him I was currently working on another project and needed a contact to another municipal office in Saudi Arabia. The man did not respond to what I had just said. A few days later, when I met with him again, he suddenly said to me, "Go visit my brother. I already told him about you." It turned out that his brother worked at the same municipal agency I wanted to do business with. I called his brother that same day and immediately got a meeting for the next day. Everything happened very fast, and this conversation also went well, because this Arab businessman was listening to me carefully and was very positive toward me. And I had the feeling, he really wanted to help me! – **Werner Piefer, German businessman. Branch: Safety Technology.**

The Arab Business Code (ABC): This classic entry into the Arab Business Club will keep occurring, on a regular basis, during your stay in the Gulf. Sometimes, without you even noticing it. We also talked about this in one of the case studies. It often seems as if the business partner is not at all interested in your needs, but actually the opposite is true. The local is seriously considering what you are saying and thinking about who the best contact for you might be. This reaction is "a reflex" people in the Gulf have. They see it almost as a responsibility they have been given – to connect people visiting their country with their extended family, those closest to them, and to recommend them to each other.

This is what Arab business people say:

> *That's right, sometimes people come to you with a kind of business, or an idea but maybe you can't help them at the moment, or it's not the type of business you are in. But if you feel comfortable with this person you need to recommend them to others, and this I will certainly do. You see, this community is very close. The people in the Gulf know each other very well.* – **Mona Almoayyed, prominent Bahraini businesswoman, member of a large family enterprise active in many business areas. Branch: Automobile, Electronics, Luxury Goods.**

Try this: Take the time, especially when you start your activity in the Gulf, to accept personal invitations from the locals, because you never really know who you are sitting across from. And also, not who this person personally knows and who they are related to, or who they can recommend you to. They could be owners of shopping malls, hotels, hospitals, construction companies, banks, telecommunication companies, oil companies, or other businesses. Maybe the people they know are managing new projects in the Gulf, which are just being set up. One project, alone, might be headed by twelve different business people, who, in turn, are owners of many other companies. The snowball effect of "everybody knows everybody" in the Gulf is immense.

Also consider: In the government there is a wide variety of local co-workers, who, in addition to their government positions, run their own small and medium sized companies. It could easily happen, during your conversation that you get an offer to work together. Or maybe to do a sponsorship.

This is what international business people say:

> *Yes, that's true. I sat across from a municipal employee and we were talking about my project. Suddenly, the young man said to me: "I could be your sponsor." At first I laughed it off – but then I noticed that he was being serious. He actually offered to work together with me.* – **German businessman. Branch: Food Industry.**

What you need to know: Always respect the people you are dealing with. Try to leave a good impression with everyone you meet! Remember to do this and never forget: This might be the key person for you – and one who could provide you with a membership into the Arab Business Club!

Unexpected entry into the Arab Business Club

> ## CASE STUDY: *Admission ticket through the father's friend*
>
> I remember a case study a friend from the Gulf told me. One day a friend of his father called him and said, "One of my acquaintances will contact you about a joint venture." My friend asked him, "Who is he?" and his father's friend said, "I don't know. But he'll call you in about two–three weeks and tell you about an exciting product." My friend asked again, "What kind of product is this?" His father's friend answered, "Don't ask me! Just meet him!" So, my friend met this man and he liked him and his product and took it on as a franchise. Later, when my friend asked his father's friend how he'd met the contact whose product he was franchising, he learned that his father's friend had just been sitting in Dubai chatting to a stranger next to him. They talked about this and that. And then this man told him he was promoting a certain product. So, they started to talk about the product and about the Arabian market. At the time, nobody was representing this product in this Gulf country. So, his father's friend exchanged numbers with this stranger. And that's how the story goes.

What makes the story of this Arab businessman from the Gulf so fascinating is that the local felt the duty to meet with the international businessman, even though he had no information about his product; and had no idea if working with him was even possible. None of this was important at that time because the local was doing it for his father's friend. This was a responsibility he had to fulfill. Just mentioning the word "father" was enough – it was a code, a "call to action" for the businessman from the Gulf.

The Arab Business Code (ABC): People in the Gulf States react to the requests of family members – without any ifs or buts. This is an unwritten law in the Gulf. Especially if the request comes from a close relative, like a father, mother, brother or sister, in which case one has to respond even more quickly. This is given a priority level of "very, very high!"

It also means the Arab business partner, who you are sitting across from, probably didn't have the time to brief himself on your product or service. Therefore, this businessman might not have any information about you or your company, as he wasn't given the time to read up on you or do the research yet. That is why you must manage your expectations in regard to your Arab business partner. Don't expect every local business person who you meet to be informed about your sphere of activity. Take personal responsibility and prepare for your meeting. Have a short presentation ready, optimally using the "Elevator Pitch" with the "Arab Business Code."

CASE STUDY: Admission ticket through the business club "in the air"

This is what Arab business people say:

> The best meeting with a new potential international business partner I ever had was in the air above Houston, Texas. The guy entered the plane and sat next to me. He was American and we were flying from Houston to New York. In the air we had three hours to discuss everything, to talk about the region and the situation of the business. And this man was the COO of one of the oil and gas companies. I was in this business as well. And then he told me, "Look, we have an office in Dubai, we have an office in Abu Dhabi, we have an office in Qatar. We need to do some work together. We produce oil and gas." And then he told me that his CEO was coming to the Gulf region and he asked me, "Would you like to meet him?" I answered, "Sure." So, I met the CEO, sat with him and took him out to show him our oil and gas company. That was the start of a number of other meetings that went very well. – **Emirati businessman, from a big business family. Branch: Oil and Gas, Food Industry.**

The Arab Business Code (ABC): The mechanics of getting admitted to the Arab Business Club operate on a different level – in places where you least expect it, like in a hotel lobby, while drinking coffee. Or at the elevator door. Or in a plane, as we heard just now in the above case study.

The same thing happened to me, several years ago: I was flying from Dubai to Doha, seated next to a Saudi businessman, who I started up a conversation with. I told him about my job. He must have liked what I did for work, because he invited me to Saudi Arabia to introduce me to some business people. He arranged for my first entry visa to Saudi Arabia, which at the time was not so easy to get, especially for an unmarried young woman like myself. But this businessman was certainly well connected and managed to procure a visa. This was the beginning of my business activity in Saudi Arabia. Today, I can say that I'm an officially recognized member of the "Arab Business Club, Special Department, Saudi Arabia."

Everybody knows everybody in the Arab Business Club – and they recommend each other, and there is always the possibility that one day they might even work together. The only thing important to the Arab businessman is that his good name, and the good name of his whole family, remains intact. He´s always keeping an eye on it and takes great care to ensure it.

Which brings me to my next point: The good reputation of the whole family must always be preserved.

Key Code 3: A good reputation comes first

This is what Arab business people say:

> *Money can come and go – but if there is a bad reputation, that's a disaster. Reputation is the most valuable thing.* – **Sheikh Nahayan Mabarak Al-Nahayan, member of the Abu Dhabi ruling family, and a businessman active in diverse areas.**

Preserving the family name is always at the forefront, everywhere, among people in the Gulf region. In their private lives but also in a business context.

Preserving a good reputation in the private sphere

It all starts with how people present themselves and meet each other in the Gulf – how one appears in public. Above all, how one behaves. Of course, it is also important how you are dressed; clothes send a strong message and determine what the society in the Gulf will think of your family. And that can be good, but also bad.

This is what Arab and international business people say:

> *When other families see my kids and they are not properly dressed, they will think, "Where are her parents? Did they not see their children, when they left the house? Do they not care about them? What kind of family*

is this?" It puts a negative reputation on my whole family's name. There-fore, I always tell my kids: "Be careful what you wear!" – **Sameera Jas-sim Fakhri, prominent Qatari businesswoman. Branch: Fashion.**

You are responsible for us! – I always tell my kids. You have to be careful that the honor and good image of our family is preserved! Always remem-ber that – no matter what you do. There must never be any disrespectful photos posted on Facebook, like for example, at parties holding a bottle of beer, or sipping wine. That is simply unacceptable! – **Sonja Ohly, Ger-man businesswoman, mother of four sheikhs from the United Arab Emirates. Branch: Communications.**

My family has built up a well-respected name. If I do something wrong, I know that will cast a black spot on my family forever. That's why I have to take care, all the time! – **Khalid S. AlNisf, well-known Kuwaiti businessman, member of a large business family active in diverse sectors.**

The Arab Business Code (ABC): A person from a Gulf State will always keep a close eye on the behavior of another person from the Gulf. It's a kind of scanning, taking in new images constantly, insert-ing them into the existing image of the reputation. And on this rests "the reputation," not only of this particular person from the Gulf, but also of his entire clan. The family protects its good name and nothing negative must ever come out in public. This is also true for business cooperation in the Gulf.

Preserving a good reputation in the business sphere

This is what Arab business people say:

What other people are saying about your business, about how you do business – that's essential. If you have a good reputation everybody will listen to you here in this country. It's like with a lady – the first thing everybody asks is: "Is she good?" That's most important, what is known about her – as well as what is known about the businessman. What his reputation is. – **Dr. Aisha Darwish Alkhemeiri from the United Arab Emirates, health professional. Branch: Medical Care.**

In the Gulf States, too, changes are evident. Some people really don't care if your actions hurt your reputation. It depends on the individual person, how he or she deals with the values and views of the world, if "losing face" is important to these people or not.

This is what Arab business people say:

> *For sure, a lot has changed, also here in the Gulf area. And there are some people from our region who are nice but never bring money to the table, or don't keep their promises. And they don't care about their reputations. But in our society, these people who are doing the wrong things will punish themselves in the long term. We're all in this world together and we know each other very well and we talk about each other all the time. We know all their bad actions and reactions. And in the long run they will not be socially accepted due to lack of respect for them – and they will feel ashamed.* – **Khalid S. AlNisf, well-known businessman of a large Kuwaiti business family, active in diverse areas.**

> *If you, for example, don't pay, that's it. The Saudi Business Community is very close knit. We know who's good or bad. It's all done by word of mouth. And if he doesn't pay, the next day he'll be out of business. No one will do business with him anymore!* – **Saudi Arabian businessman, active in diverse fields of business.**

The Arab Business Code (ABC): Especially for recognized family clans, preserving a good name and avoiding shame is very important. This is also something I've noticed in my years of observing people from the Gulf States. Business people of the Gulf are very careful when it comes to their choice of international business partners, because their sound reputation, and that of the entire tribe, must not be damaged in any way. They will take all appropriate measures to find out more about the international business partners. Above all, they will find out if they have a good reputation.

How business people in the gulf protect their reputations

Arab business people "x-ray" their counterparts in detail – they do in depth research on the international business partner and their company and make use of their extensive network to learn more about them.

CASE STUDY: *A Google search*

This is what Arab business people say:

> *It's so important with whom you associate. I remember a very powerful international business personality, quite famous. But when I Googled him, I found out that he had stock market issues, serious*

stock market related problems. So, I told myself that I obviously don't want a relationship with him. And immediately I ignored his emails and did not continue our relationship, hoping that it would eventually die out. But he continued, and I let him know that I had checked on him and there were things I was concerned about. I explained to him, "Look, our association would not look good to the other people I have business dealings with. I have maybe one business with you that might turn out OK, but that's a risk for me." And that was the end of it. – **Omani businessman, active in diverse areas. Branch: Oil and Gas, Manufacturing, Mining.**

The Arab Business Code (ABC): A bad reputation sticks to a person in the Gulf region like "super glue." You can be sure that, as soon as the international business man has left his office, the Arab businessman will look at the business card and figuratively "x-ray" it, studying every last detail. He'll use all his resources and also involve his employees in the process to thoroughly research everything about the man. He, himself, will Google this person. People from the Gulf love to Google, a lot. And then he will take a look, step by step, at where this man is from, his background, his career, and if he has any professional contacts already. If that's the case, he'll turn to his family network and, with the help of his family members, continue probing. From all this information, he forms a general picture about the international businessman. And he'll ask himself, "Do I really want to do business with this person? And, above all: Is there anything in his past that could damage my good name or the reputation of my family?"

This is what Arab business people say:

We don't sit easily with a company. We really review them before we meet them, their owners or representatives. We know about their cases; we review their transparency – we know everything about them. Especially their reputation is very important for us to know. – **Dr. Abdulrahman Alzamil, prominent Saudi Arabian involved in a big family business, active in diverse areas.**

Since reputation is so important for business people, let us examine the dynamics of reputation more closely. Especially the chances, but also the dangers this entails.

Opportunities for achieving a good reputation

This is what Arab business people say:

> *We don't forget! People will talk about you. And one day also the leadership of the country will know about you.* – **Badria Almulla, prominent businesswoman from a big business family of the United Arab Emirates, active in diverse fields of business.**

CASE STUDY: *Finally – a business success!*

This is what international business people say:

> *I had an experience like that. Although I had great talks with an Arab businessman in the Gulf, I never got a contract from him. Five years later, out of the blue, someone approached me and offered me a project in Dubai. A few weeks later I ran into the businessman I'd met five years ago – the one I had great talks with, but that never ended in a business deal. We began to speak about the project in Dubai. And then he just said to me, as an aside, "Well, who do you think got you the job." Immediately it became clear to me: he was responsible for me getting this deal – after five years! Because he was involved in the project. And since he'd kept a close eye on me and my work over the years and knew what I was doing, he recommended me to his partner.* – **German businessman, active in diverse fields of business.**

The Arab Business Code (ABC): That's the good news from the Gulf – word travels at the right time. You'll be recommended. Arab business people never forget anything! They're known for their excellent memories, have a brilliant archiving system – especially when it comes to good reputations of international business people. If you've made a positive impression, they'll contact you one day.

This is what Arab business people say:

> *All the good things will be rewarded! To any company who builds a good reputation for their name. Maybe they won't be rewarded right away, but they'll be paid back in the future. That's for sure.* – **Ahmad Almutlaq, well-known Saudi Arabian businessman, active in diverse fields of business.**

Causes of a bad reputation – losing face: opportunities and risks

What you need to know: There are all kinds of actions that can damage the reputation of an Arab businessman and his entire family. One of the worst things is "losing face" – when the Arab businessman's reputation is injured, when he's put down, in his own society, as a "loser" or "liar."

Let us take a closer look at this "losing face." It can happen in different ways, on diverse levels and, have various impacts.

Level 1 – Losing face "one-on-one"

Situation: Even if only two business people are sitting across from each other in a meeting, one of them could lose face. In such "intimate" situations, we can speak of a low level of losing face.

CASE STUDY: *Uncovered lies – the person is identified as a liar*

This is what international business people say:

I had a project that needed financing. I thought I had found it in a big Arab company in Dubai and scheduled an appointment with the head of the company, even though it was during Ramadan, the time of fasting. Waiting patiently for 45 minutes was nothing out of the norm. When I was finally called into his office, I began my presentation, explaining why the project was so important and how potential partners could profit from it, in a business sense. Then the telephone rang. The Arab businessman excused himself and picked up the phone. "These things happen," I thought, trying to be tolerant.

What my counterpart did not know was that I had learned Arabic and could understand what he was saying. I heard him tell someone in Arabic, "I can't come to iftar tonight, I'm going to my mother's for iftar." Iftar is the first meal after breaking the fast that people eat together. The Arab businessman said goodbye on the phone and apologized, politely for the interruption. I nodded, sympathetically, and continued with my "little talk," my presentation. Again, the phone rang. He apologized politely, looked at the caller number and explained that he really had to take this call, that it was very important for him. Again, I nodded empathetically. The businessman picked up and I heard him say to his mother, in Arabic, "Mama, I can't come to iftar tonight, I'm sorry. I have a very,

very important meeting. I'm really very, very, sorry." Well, I thought, lying during the fast – was that really appropriate? But of course, I didn't say anything. The Arab businessman said goodbye to his mother. And, again after ending the phone call, he told me that he was sorry but that the call couldn't wait. He asked me to continue with my presentation. And that's exactly what I did – but it didn't even take five minutes for the phone to ring once more. And, again, the businessman picked up. This time it seemed his girlfriend was on the line, because he said, "Darling, it's not a problem. I'm free tonight and we can meet up!" Well, that was too much for me. I got up, collected my documents and said in Arabic, "Call me when you want to talk business again." Instantly, the Arab businessman's jaw dropped and his face turned bright red. He hadn't expected this.

Now, it just so happened that at the time I was also on the board of the German Business Council and often attended official functions. About two weeks later, at one such event, I spotted this Arab business-man coming out of the elevator. And when he saw me standing in the greeting line, in a second he turned around and left the reception. He was embarrassed that I had caused him to lose face. – **Sonja Ohly, German businesswoman and mother of four sheikhs from the United Arab Emirates. Branch: Communication.**

What you need to know: From that moment on, that particular Arab businessman will do everything in his power to avoid the business-woman, whenever their paths might cross. That, in itself, is an unpleas-ant situation. However, what's especially damaging to business in this "unresolved relationship" is that the man will not want to see this busi-nesswoman in any social setting anymore. And by "any social setting," I mean the entire community in the Gulf. Because, if they meet by chance, the businessman's embarrassing behavior might come to light, the fact that he lied – especially during the holy fast, which made it even worse.

Of course, the businessman will never directly badmouth the busi-nesswoman. This does not go over well in Gulf society and would also be too conspicuous. But what he most certainly will do is to inter-ject arguments and hints to indirectly influence the men and women around him. These people, in turn, will begin to wonder if it's wise to do business with this woman in the future, or even to see her again. As already mentioned, these arguments will be slipped into the conver-sation, very diplomatically of course, finely packed into little remarks. And naturally, between the lines, totally in the manner of Arab Com-munication Culture.

The more esteemed and powerful the businessman in the Gulf community is, the worse the business consequences of the one-on-one loss of face are for the international business person, because the local's hints and suggestions will resonate more and also be acted upon. The outcome: step by step, at first maybe not even noticeably, the business-woman will be pushed out of the "Business Club in the Gulf." This will happen slowly, it's a drawn-out process. She'll get fewer and fewer invitations. And soon she won't be involved in community life in the Gulf anymore.

In our case study the businesswoman was lucky and the Arab businessman she met with was not such a distinguished person. And since she herself was married to a member of a ruling family, she could quickly position her good reputation in the "big family network." But that's a special case and not a risk one should take!

So, when you're sitting across from an Arab partner, always consider the danger of damaging his or her reputation. Keep this story in mind and bite your tongue before you express, as in our case study, direct criticism, thereby causing the person to "lose face" because an Arab business person will find it very hard to forgive you. Even if it's only a single remark, "a slip up" like this entails a lot of cleanup work. You'll have to invest lots of time, energy and money in rebuilding a relationship of trust to the Arab partner. Keep in mind: Arab business people are not particularly trained in giving and receiving feedback and these kinds of insults cannot be as quickly and directly talked through in the Gulf as in other parts of the world. If you run into a situation like this, repairing the damage will simply take plenty of time.

Try this: Actively call to mind this case study, especially when you're feeling impatient. Smile and tell yourself, "This will definitely not happen to me! Absolutely not!" Keep saying that over and over again, when the "Incensed Anger Rascal" inside you pops up, a creature on the verge of an eruption, like a volcano.

But, as I said, this example only demonstrates a low level of losing face. Of course, this can reach higher levels, especially if you cause the Arab businessman to lose face in front of third parties – if you express direct insults in front of third parties, or you behave in a way that leads to the Arab business person losing face in a group. Let's look into this.

Level 2: "Indirectly" losing face in a group

We speak of this situation when international business people cause an Arab businessman to lose face, without directly addressing him, but still embarrassing him in front of the group. This can lead to the Arab businessman being labeled a "loser" and bad businessman in his own circles. And it guarantees a subsequent avoidance reaction by the Arab businessman; followed by the immediate termination of all business ties with the international business partner.

CASE STUDY: *Keeping customer dissatisfaction – a secret leads to a business breakup*

An international businesswoman founded a company in Doha, together with a businessman from the Gulf. At first, both parties presented a united front. They were euphoric, promoted each other, even at official functions. It was obvious the goal was successful cooperation. And the Arab businessman, himself, did everything in his power and opened all doors for the businesswoman. He put her into contact with the most distinguished business people in the Gulf. In this way, he brought in many commissions – through friends, relatives, and acquaintances – for the newly founded company. It seemed perfect.

But, behind the scenes it became increasingly apparent that the businesswoman was not doing her job professionally. The promises she made to clients were not being kept. There were many problems with deliveries and complaints, and the customers were growing more and more dissatisfied. But the Arab businessman heard nothing about this. Inside his social circle, people were beginning to wonder why he'd made this woman his business partner, for he was considered a successful businessman. Gradually, the orders began to lessen. At some point, another Arab businessman conveyed the customer's dissatisfaction to the local, by saying, "Your new company is doing very unprofessional work, your customers are very dissatisfied. Watch out! It's damaging your reputation." This hit home – the Arab businessman took immediate action. The very next day he ended his cooperation with the businesswoman. The day after that, the local newspapers reported that this businessman had cut all business ties to the international businesswoman and that they would not work together in future.

What you need to know: From this case study you can see that the Arab businessman was very positive about working together in the beginning. He was convinced he and the businesswoman would be successful, otherwise he never would have put so much effort into it.

If the businesswoman had informed him of the difficulties early on, this situation wouldn't have escalated. Then the Arab businessman would've been able to take other measures. Not disclosing the problem was clearly the wrong approach and culminated in the Arab business-man "losing face" in his own community. This damage to reputation forced the Arab businessman to take action in a kind of state of emer-gency way. Because she had broken a "code," crossed a psychological line for the Arab businessman and attacked him in the professional sphere of his life, she damaged his good name as a respected, success-ful businessman in his own community. What made it even worse was the fact that the Arab businessman had not even noticed the damage to his reputation for quite some time. But when he realized this, he reacted promptly and took drastic measures, by immediately "stepping on the brakes" and announcing in a newspaper article that he was dis-tancing himself from her.

This, by the way, is a typical "reflex" of Arab business people from the Gulf. When they've made a decision, they act with a finality that is not really understandable to the outside world. This is a line they must immediately draw, so that they can "put things in order" again.

Business people from the Gulf actually have a very hard time sepa-rating from something, be it a property or a business partner. They are known for their loyalty and long-term commitment. But when their reputations are at stake, these values don't come into play. Their reac-tions are instantaneous and final.

The Arab Business Code (ABC): Arab business people from the Gulf cannot accept being labeled "losers" in their community, in their country.

This is what Arab business people say:

And that's what you need to know about us, the opposite side: when I'm getting into an agreement with someone, an international company, it's all recognized by my country, my people that there is a company pre-sented by this particular Omani – me. And if anything bad happens, it will ruin my reputation in my country. That's really the worst thing that can happen to me! – **Issa Alrawahi, well-known businessman from Oman. Branch: Oil and Gas Industry.**

If you trust somebody and he does not deliver – you have a problem. Because they can leave your country, but you cannot run away. And you have a reputation to lose. – **Sherida Saad Jubran Al-Kaabi, promi-nent Qatari businessman, active in many areas of business.**

Try this: Empathize with the people from the Gulf. Try to imagine how you would react if every one of your actions was carefully observed by a group. And how it makes a businessman feel if he can't keep his promise, how humiliating that must be for him and how badly his position in society is affected by this. Then be very aware that he, a local, cannot just "pack up and leave" the Gulf, escape abroad and start a new life. If for no other reason, this is not possible because of family affiliations and his responsibility to his clan.

That's why you should think about how your remarks and actions strengthen the Arab business partner's standing in society, how you can promote his good reputation.

As we're now on the subject of "empathizing with the Arab businessman," let's take it a step further. The next case study demonstrates the consequences of losing face in the community. It should help you better understand the mindset of the Arab business person.

CASE STUDY: *Shame in one's own community; no more visiting the* Diwan

A Kuwaiti businessman had invested in a listed company. This Kuwaiti was a role model for business people in the Arab world. People admired him for having the courage to invest in this enterprise. It was greatly discussed amongst people in the *Diwan* (the place of sitting), but also with the Kuwaiti himself, because he was there every day and liked to talk about his business successes. Then came the moment when the company totally dropped on the stock market. And from that day on, the Kuwaiti no longer visited the *Diwan*. He was so embarrassed to have failed before the eyes of the other Kuwaitis.

Before we conclude this topic, I'd like to introduce another degree of possible loss of face in the Arab region, namely, if a businessman is insulted verbally. Here we are dealing with a direct voicing of an insult in front of other people. This is the highest level of losing face.

Level 3: "Direct" loss of face in the group

Situation: During a business meeting with many participants, an international businessman tells his Arab counterpart his honest opinion in a form, or as a remark, that appears insulting. The presence of the group sets off the process of "losing face" and the reaction of the Arab business people is justifiably strong, much more emotional, because it is an even greater embarrassment in front of an audience. This makes the Arab businessman feel totally cornered, and his reaction will be accordingly harsh.

CASE STUDY: *When an Arab businessman loses his self-control – an explosion of anger*

This is what international business people say:

> We had finally negotiated a fixed contract about the conditions of launching the new project. The financing conditions were also part of the contract. Everything had been decided already. At the next meeting, our Arab business partner suddenly began to speak about how he imagined the financial process would look. And that this could take time, many years. He spoke about it as if we were still at the early stages of negotiating the points in the contract. We listened to this for a while and said nothing. But then a member of the inter-national team, who was completely upset, burst out with, "What's this supposed to mean? There's already a legally valid. contract in place! And everything about the financing is already clearly stated in it. So, why are you beating about the bush?" Instantly, the Arab business partner withdrew physically, his eyes literally popped out, and his lips began to quiver. You could tell he'd reached a point where he couldn't hold back his anger. Then he yelled at the speaker in front of the whole group – and told him how dare he talk to him like that. This was followed by a tirade and a flood of furious words that lasted over twenty minutes. Finally, the Arab businessman got up and said goodbye with these words: "I'll have nothing more to do with this project! Please send me all the necessary paperwork, so that we can end this fairly!" – **Austrian businessman, active in many areas of business.**

And now it's time for a little break – to lean back, and carefully exam-ine the situation. Let's not focus on who's right or wrong in this case. I'd like to concentrate more on the dynamics of the communica-tion process, whereby the Arab businessman felt attacked in front of an audience and was thereby pushed into an outsider position. This businessman reacted with an outburst of rage, in a very extroverted way, which, basically, is still not the norm in the Gulf. Usually, in a situation like that the "Exit Strategy According to the Arab Business Code" is applied. Arab people diplomatically and politely retreat after such remarks. One never hears from them again, and they are impossible to contact.

The businessman in this case study shows what's going on inside him. He displays weakness, vulnerability – that's doubly embarrassing for proud Arab businessmen. Then the fit of anger in front of the whole group – bringing us into the realm of a so-called double loss of face, as defined by the Arab Business Code.

What can be done after such a "slip up?" How is one supposed to react? Can this situation be saved, and if so, how?

My many years of observation and conversations have brought me to the realization that in situations like this there really is only one recommended technique. I call it the "stunning honesty toward Arab businessmen" approach. It's a kind of damage control, that can be applied on a long-term basis.

The technique of "stunning honesty" after a double loss of face: saving what can still be saved

This technique covers two different aspects and, if possible, a two-step program needs to be implemented. If only one step is doable, then only use one.

Step 1: Using the "third man" approach – please take over!

Here a third party serves as mediator between the actual trigger of the situation, the person who started it all, and the Arab businessman. Just some short background: in every group there is usually at least one person who has a good rapport with the Arab counterpart, or very good personal access. I call this person the "third man," but of course this person can also be a woman. What's important here is that the group identify this individual and that the "third man" take action on the very day of the incident and contact the Arab businessman, preferably by phone.

This is what international business people say:

When a colleague verbally insulted an Arab counterpart in a meeting, I took on the role of the "third man," because in previous meetings I'd gotten along well with this Arab businessman. I called him on his mobile phone that same evening. He didn't answer his phone that evening, but that didn't surprise me. I could tell that he was still angry and had to

*work through this incident for himself. What I did though, was send him
a text message that evening, asking him for a quick chat: "Just give me
five to ten minutes of your time – I don't need more," I wrote to him.
The next day I called again – this time he picked up. He was still very
upset by the incident. I listened to him calmly and then told him that
I understood his side and that he was right in this matter. In passing, I
explained that the employee in question was still a bit young, rash, and
that was why he went too far. After that we talked of other things and
then said goodbye. We agreed to meet two weeks later.* – **Heinz Palme,
Austrian businessman. Branch: Sports and Leisure.**

The Arab Business Code (ABC): This "third man" is, very professionally, using the Gas-Shift-Brake technique. At first, he "steps on the
gas" by taking the initiative and calling the businessman. This is a way
of declaring his respect for the Arab businessman. It is perfectly clear
to the mediator that the businessman will not pick up right away. He
understands that a proud Arab businessman, whose honor has been so
severely wounded, cannot simply communicate with someone a few
hours later. And he respects this by "taking his foot off the accelerator"
and, so to speak, shifting to a lower gear – in the form of a text message
with a nonverbal message of, "You are important to me and I will keep
at it." He knows his counterpart can read between the lines, and that
he will interpret his short text in this way. When there's no reaction
to his second attempt to communicate, the "third man" also respects
this and immediately "steps on the brakes." For, he knows, tomorrow
is another day and he can begin this ritual all over again. Once more,
using the Gas-Shift-Brake technique, to keep things in balance.

After these kinds of slip ups with Arab business people, the "third
man" or "third woman" needs to have great sensitivity and tact and
also manage their expectations with regard to the Arab business person. Because herein lies the stumbling block for overzealous mediators,
who might have the best intentions at a particular wrong moment.
For example, they might want to smooth it over that same evening,
which often does not work out well. Constant "pressure calls" are also
counterproductive. This makes the person feel even more cornered and
they are apt to totally withdraw. And that's when things get really complicated. That's why this first contact is a balancing act for the "third
man," a continuous hanging on and letting go, and why the Gas-Shift-
Brake technique is very helpful here.

If the mediator, the "third man," manages to do a good job as a
pathfinder, then the second step (Step 2) can be applied: The personal

apology. This has to come directly from the "aggressor," the person who triggered the conflict leading to a loss of face. Here too, proceed with utmost delicacy and choose the right form of apology. Depending on the situation, there are different options here. I would like to present two of them.

1. The written apology

When it comes to big slip ups, one should let some time pass after the incident. In talks with business people, they suggested a timeframe of one week to ten days before offering the apology. And this should, preferably, be done in writing, because then the Arab businessman has time to let the written message work on him. The focal point should be an atmosphere of, "I'm sorry."

An example of an apology letter on the basis of the Arab Business Code (ABC)

Dear Mohammed,

A few days have gone by. I would like to apologize to you. I know that the way I behaved was not appropriate. But please understand that I have invested a lot of passion in this project and its success is of great personal importance to me. I thank you for all the support you've given me in developing this project and for all the opportunities you've opened for me. We've achieved a lot together and I'd like to continue to do so in the future. I hope you'll give me the opportunity to speak personally to you.

After writing a letter like this there is only one thing to do: be patient and wait it out! And when some time has passed, initiate contact again, continue by reapplying the Gas-Shift-Brake technique.

I can even tell you how the Arab businessman from our previous case study reacted to this letter. Upon receiving it he thought: "It's a very nice gesture, that he's written to me!" After writing the letter, the person who started the conflict let it rest, he "let go" and did not contact the Arab businessman until more than half a year had passed. Then he began again, with new attempts at reaching out, and looked for places where the businessman regularly went, like "the place of sitting." With each encounter the relationship improved, step by step. A friendship blossomed. A year later the two men were working together again.

2. The immediate verbal apology

Sometimes, you need to react directly when it happens – immediately – the very moment you make an insulting remark. Or if you're stuck in an aggressive discussion with your Arab counterpart, you must pull the brake and apologize for your verbal slip by being "stunningly honest." Although this may cause you to lose face in the group, it is necessary. Then you must show you are genuinely interested in continuing the business relationship. It's the only option. Here too, I suggest the Gas-Shift-Brake technique combined with the right choice of words.

This is what international business people say:

If, during a meeting, I "slip up" with an insulting remark – then I immediately, in that very moment, I say, "Sorry! I was being too harsh, I wasn't thinking!" In doing so, I look the local straight in the eye, with great respect. That is the only way to save this meeting. – **Jean-Pierre Simon, Swiss manager. Branch: Hospitality Industry.**

Try this: In such a situation, imagine you've just stepped on a patch of ice and by frantically "scuttling around" you lose your balance even more. It's time to calm down – visualize this for yourself. After an insulting remark, you have to get your balance with your counterpart back and that can only happen if you bring the calm back into the talks. Only then can you pay your business partner the necessary respect. Remember, an open confrontation with an Arab business person, in front of an audience is counterproductive, even if you mean well and only want to be honest – and even if you are right. In moments like this, try listening with respect to your Arab counterpart.

This is what international business people say:

Aggressive objections in a meeting with Arab business people achieve nothing, even if the rage is at a boiling point. Because that only adds more fuel to the fire. This is something I have learned. Before, I used to react differently – I presented counter arguments and opened a discussion – also in the presence of third parties, because I was right and wanted to put it all out on the table. But that made Arab business people, especially in the top positions, even more angry. That's why I stopped. Today, I can listen calmly and also agree with Arab counterparts. I never give a clear "yes" to things I know I won't be able to comply with. In situations like this I always say, "I'll do my best" and that calms down the whole situation. – **Austrian businessman, Branch: Infrastructure Projects.**

In short, wait until the volcanic eruption has died down! And, above all, don't let yourself be manipulated by "Paralyzing Fear!" It's one of our characters of the "Emotional Hinderers in the Gulf" (See Appendix on Emotional Hinderers). And don't forget, at some point it will be over and a new time will come, because, in principle, you can always go back to the Arab business person. It will take some time, but if you have not done serious damage to your relationship with your Arab business partner, he or she will always take you back. The "big family" of the Arab Gulf keeps an eye out for one another.

How to use the power of "reputation" to manage local employees

Losing face as a positive management tool: smart strategies for managing local employees

For years, international companies with subcontractors or sites in the Gulf States had to comply with the nationalization contingent. This stipulation by local governments is called Qatarization, Emiratization, Saudization, Kuwaitization, Omanization – which means that international companies in the region have to recruit a certain percentage of employees from the local workforce. Experts predict that this percentage will increase in future.

In the meantime, the experience of companies with this has shown that, besides success stories, there are also quite a few cases of dissatisfaction on both sides. One of the claims the companies make is that the locals are disinterested and lack an enthusiastic attitude toward work. Some companies even describe the behavior of their employees as damaging to business. The side of the Arab employees complains about insufficient pay in relation to the working hours and compared to the employment contracts of government officials in the Gulf. Another disappointment for local employees is the supposed lack of future prospects.

This was reason enough for me and my team to examine this issue in more depth. We posed the question: How can the management of expectations, on both sides, be improved? We also looked into what could motivate this new generation of local employees, socially and emotionally, to be more engaged in their work – something that could bring more job satisfaction. That's why we worked closely with international and Arab business people on developing techniques to support satisfactory cooperation. And we had a clear goal: to reach a win-win solution for both sides.

In line with this chapter's information on "losing face," I want to demonstrate a technique that Arab business people use with their own compatriots, and employees from the Gulf region.

But first, let us examine a case study and compare the actions of international managers with those of Arab managers. How they would act in such a situation.

CASE STUDY: *Local employees try to take advantage by using "family" as an excuse*

A local employee who worked at a western company in the Gulf went to the western manager and told him, "I have to take my mother to the hospital. The doctor was just with her. Please let me go now. It's really urgent!" The manager, who was British, told his employee, "I'm terribly sorry, but you have to take a personal day for this, or provide some sort of evidence that you are telling the truth. Otherwise, I can't let you go." The employee could not come up with the requested proof, and also did not take a day off for this. So, the manager didn't allow him to leave. This resulted in the employee being physically present, but, as attested by the way he worked that day, not at all motivated. He only did the bare minimum and was totally disinterested. He kept making mistakes that harmed the business, but which the manager could not directly prove. Therefore, he had no reason to fire him, no concrete proof for dismissal.

How would an Arab Business manager deal with this situation?

This is what Arab business people say:

You see, I wouldn't ask for any note, even if I knew the employee was lying to me. I'd just say, "OK, take care of your mother," and then I'd let him go. I'd ask my assistant to give him a call in two hours to ask about his mother, then I'd leave him in peace. In a week, when he was back at work, I'd ask him, "How's your mother?" And if he'd been lying, he wouldn't be able to say what she had suffered from, a fever or whatever. And if I knew from his answer to my questions that he wasn't telling the truth, I'd write a text message asking how his mother was and to which hospital she had been brought. If he answered, "I took her to hospital X," I would get back to him with, "That's not a good hospital, have her transferred to hospital Y." You see, with all that correspondence I would indirectly send him the message: "You are lying to me and I know it." And I would continue to ask about his mother's health. From the way I keep on communicating with him, he'd know that I knew something. He might get nervous, but he wouldn't talk about it – you get my point? It would certainly make him think and put him off from doing something like this to me again! – **Ibrahim Alkindi, well-known businessman from the United Arab Emirates, active in many business areas.**

What you need to know: This local manager did not let himself be manipulated by the employee, even through the dynamics of family. He had respect for the employee's need for time off to deal with the problem of a close family member, his mother. But, because of the way his employee behaved, he wasn't sure if he was telling the truth. He needed to check up on this – by testing him, now and then, with the help of "Communication Culture on the Basis of the Arab Business Code" (Chapter 5). When he was certain the employee had lied, he applied the tool of "indirect loss of face" with the message: "I caught you in a lie! Be careful! I'm watching you! Constantly!" And, throughout all this, the local manager from the Gulf always made sure to show great respect for the dynamics of family.

Never forget the Arab Business Code (ABC): The family comes first in these countries. You must also respect this notion in regard to your local employees in the Gulf. It doesn't make sense to deny employees time off when their close family members, like mothers or fathers, are sick. So, at this point you might be thinking: "What will this lead to? Everyone will take time off, then there will be no one left to work here!" Not everyone will leave, and different cultures have different customs – that's why this book exists. Just have in mind: there isn't a lot to be gained from a local employee with his "head down," just standing around the workplace, about to make some mistakes that might hurt business, due to his nervousness, lack of concentration, or frustration with the company. That's why, when it comes to managing local employees, one needs to have smart tactics and great skill and sensitivity. This does not mean that you allow yourself to be lied to by local employees. By no means. So, try the following.

Two-step program of strategic employee management with the Arab Business Code (ABC)

First: Find out the truth about your employee by indirectly challenging him. The public loss of face in the form of "bring me the document or I won't trust you," is a rough insult. And, by doing so you make it clear, from the very beginning, that you think your employee is a liar.

Act like the local manager – give the employee the benefit of the doubt, take a leap of faith, and place him under observation. Make sure he's aware of this, indirectly, by sending little messages through your learned communication culture skills on the basis of the Arab Gulf Code. This is something you can practice, and get better at, with time.

Second: If you've caught him in a lie, give him more work to do. In this way you are challenging him to concentrate on his job. Try it and see what happens!

Tools for successful reputation management

Today, as in the past, word of mouth is a time-tested communication tool in the Gulf. It brings with it certain dynamics and an operating principle that no PR campaign anywhere in the world can equal. In the past few years, a second tool has been successfully developed, in addition to the traditional verbal means, namely, "word of mouth via social media." This tool can also be very effective in building reputations in the Gulf.

Tool 1: Dynamics of traditional "word of mouth" recommendations

We've already discussed, in individual chapters, how great the communication hub of "the place of sitting" is. It's a place where people in the Gulf region meet regularly to chat and exchange news – naturally about international business people as well! In the UAE this special place is called the *Majlis* and in Kuwait or Saudi Arabia it's known as *the Diwan*. This is where local business people from the Gulf come together and collect additional information about international companies, so they can form an "overall picture" and get more insight into the companies' reputations. And it can be positive, but also negative.

This is what Arab business people say:

> *Here in the community, our conversations are your advertisement – we talk with each other a lot, especially in our region and a lot in my industry, the fast food business. We meet regularly in the Diwan. And when people like my food, they ask about my product and with whom I'm working. If I say, "This international businessman is a great partner – really good to work with," then people will trust my evaluation and take in the good reputation of this businessman. And one day they will get in touch with him. But it can also be the other way around. I remember I once bought a machine in Germany, it cost around €50,000. After two months the machine didn't work anymore, there was a leak in the tank. But there was nobody in the area who could repair it, so we had to wait. The machine was broken for three months. Finally, the manufacturer came, but even then, they couldn't repair it, as it was an old model. They suggested I purchase a new model. But I didn't want to pay – I*

just wanted to have the machine I had already bought working. It still doesn't work. And if anyone asks me about this company you can be sure I'll advise them and I'll tell them, "Never work with them!" – **Salah H. Sobghan, well-known Saudi Arabian businessman. Branch: Food Industry.**

It's normal in the Diwan that people ask you about certain names. What do you know about them? What do you know about their company and their business? We always ask about each other. That's how we create trust. – **Khalid S. AlNisf, prominent businessman from Kuwait, active in many areas of business.**

What you need to know: You might be thinking that "word of mouth" is mostly a tool for the older generation; young people are more involved in social media. But that's where you're wrong! Many young business people from the Gulf regularly go to "the place of sitting" and realize the great potential to promote their reputations there.

This is what younger Arab business people say:

We cannot just depend on social media. You can be sure that actual word of mouth gets out to at least ten other people. Even for us, the young generation in Qatar, this word of mouth travels faster than social media. Faster than any possible channel. – **Ibrahim M. Hassan Naqi Al-Emadi, well-known Qatari businessman. Branch: Hospitality Industry.**

Try this: Regularly go to the "places of sitting" and mention your success stories there. Talk about your current accomplishments. Every Arab businessman is interested in success stories, especially people in the Gulf. They are inspired to tell other Arab business people about this. And that's how a PR campaign with the Arab Business Code works. You won't have to spend a cent – and it will do wonders for your reputation.

Keep in mind: You need to build your reputation, promoting presentations in "the place of sitting." First, make a list of all your positive aspects, and those of your company, and formulate short and interesting stories or anecdotes about them. Even if Arab business people would love to listen to you for hours on end, they simply can't keep track of all the stories. So only tell the best stories. Remember this and develop your own short stories which are worth retelling to others.

Tool 2: Word of mouth through social media

This is what Arab business people say:

Social media is another very effective way to spread word of mouth! As all of us are connected via Twitter or Facebook, we can tell each other really quickly, "Don't buy this – it's cheap quality," or, "Don't go to that restaurant" – it creates a certain reputation for places, products and people in the Gulf quickly. – **Faisal Almahroos, well-known Bahraini businessman. Branches: Oil and Gas Industry.**

With social media they're sharing with us their life and experiences. It's almost like a real movie. What's interesting – you can also find small and medium sized businesses there. And some of them have really good ideas! Interesting for special investments. – **Ahmed Alzamil, businessman from a big Saudi Arabian business family, active in diverse areas.**

The Arabian Gulf uses social media intensely. These dynamics have also been used by corporations and companies to reach their target group through strong promotion. Their success has proven them right – it's not uncommon to have a million followers. And thus, social media activities generate commercial success.

Due to these methods, there are also smaller businesses in the Gulf that have fully withdrawn from classic modes of advertising and now exclusively use social channels to build up their reputations and, thereby, succeed in business. I'm thinking of the success story of the Surf House in Dubai where you could not only surf, but also drink coffee and buy surf wear. With 7,000 followers, the Surf House reached a direct target group on Facebook and Instagram. In a very short time, they could directly address 12,000 followers. In this way, the company could conduct direct marketing on a regular basis – a priceless feat that significantly contributed to commercial success.

Nevertheless, social media also has a flip side. People need to be aware of the hidden dangers and stumbling blocks if these virtual platforms are used in the wrong way. If you're not careful you could injure your reputation and get the opposite result: a damaged reputation.

So, prepare yourself well for building up a good reputation through social media! First, make sure this communication instrument suits you. Only after you have made that decision, can you think through your strategy and work out a masterplan with the individual steps.

And since we're talking about measures to promote your reputation, I'd like to turn to a type of personality that is of particular importance in this context: "The Influencer" – and how they act within the framework of the Arab Business Code. Here, we are speaking of testimonials, credible people (men and women) who can say positive things about you, your company or your product on social media. In the following pages I'd like to explain the importance of these influencers who are well versed in the Arab Business Code.

Tool 3: Dynamics of virtual reputation promoters – influencers and the Arab Business Code (ABC)

Influencers are people who, due to their strong presence and high standing in social platforms, have built up a relationship of trust to a mass audience. These people are trusted – that's why they can boost the reputation of the product, service or person they advertise or recommend. In the Arab Gulf, too, there are influencers who have built up a faithful following in social networks.

Influencers who master the Arab Business Code can be prominent soccer players, race car drivers, or journalists of the region, or they are simply held in high esteem in their communities. All of them are role models of their generation, who have made a good name for themselves in the Gulf and are therefore trustworthy, because if they make misleading statements or bad recommendations, they could lose their own reputation.

How do influencers manage to build a good reputation by using the Arab Business Code (ABC)?

What differentiates these kinds of influencers from influencers in the rest of the world, is that they know exactly how to communicate with their own people, the local target group. They know how far they can go with their remarks, which "key words" the people in the Gulf region will respond to. They grew up with the Arab Business Code, so they are especially good at it.

Local influencers from the Gulf also have the same business model, as their colleagues worldwide, namely, recommendations. They interact with their followers regularly, they recommend products, food, cosmetics, hotels. The list is endless. Companies understand the value of these virtual word of mouth recommendations and that success in the Gulf is only possible with a good reputation!

This is what Arab business people say:

With one famous guy your business can be supported a lot. For example, we had a boutique hotel and one of the influencers had a small party in the ballroom. After that, for the next couple of months, the ballroom was reserved for parties all the time by different categories of people around the city! – **Bander Alzamil, businessman of a large Saudi Arabian business family, active in diverse areas.**

On the subject of influencers there is much more to be said; their tactics are fascinating. In the course of our research, we've closely observed this segment of the market. But there is another aspect I'd like to address because it's crucial for promoting reputations of international business people in the Gulf. And what makes the whole thing even better – it saves you money. Here we are dealing with "the shame effect" of the family mechanism. Local influencers know exactly how to apply this special effect into the Arab Business Code. As a result, they communicate for free.

This is what Arab business people say:

When I, as a local businessman partner, together with an international company, for example, open a business with a special brand name in Qatar – then you can be sure that one of the members of my large family is an influencer. And this person is given the responsibility of posting several things for free. Because he's a member of my family, so for him it's a must. You have to support the family! And if you don't support them – it brings shame on the whole family. – **Qatari businessman, active in diverse areas of business.**

Something to consider: It's an unwritten rule that families stick together, even when it comes to advertising in social media! Of course, there might be disagreements in individual families. Naturally, everything has to be above board and adjusted to the legal conditions, but the basic principle is that one has to support the other in developing business. If you don't do this, the "shame effect" kicks in – and you bring shame on yourself and the entire family.

Another unwritten rule for people in the Gulf is that there has to be an equal amount of "give and take." The local influencer mentioned above will also, one day, turn to his relative, the Arab businessman, when he needs something. These tradeoffs are made among themselves, a balance is preserved, as it should be in every successful relationship.

Try this: Simply ask your Arab business partner if there is an influencer in his family clan, or maybe among his circle of friends and acquaintances. You know that everybody knows everybody in the Gulf. And somewhere there is sure to be a local influencer, fluent in the Arab

Business Code, who can support you and your local business partner in achieving and maintaining a good reputation in the Gulf.

Key Code 4 – Meaning of hierarchies

Social structures and hierarchies play a role everywhere in the world but in the Gulf States they are absolutely crucial for business success. The older and wiser are appreciated with great respect and it is often these elders who sit, hierarchically, at the very top of corporate empires and in high government positions and therefore also make the final decisions in business.

Psyche of the decision maker

To understand the character make up of Arab business decision makers we have to go back in time – to the desert. Let's examine a desert tribal leader from a psychological point of view: how was he feeling as he wandered through the desert with his tribe? What effect did the endless stretches of desert have on him? How did he find his orientation back then? With the help of nature or his instinct? There were no signposts in the desert back then, and no iPhones to search Google Maps and find your location. The desert people had to have great faith in themselves; the job of tribal leader was not for anxious or fearful people. Yesterday's tribal leaders were the strong characters of their time.

Today, you can still encounter these charismatic, strong willed bosses in the Arabian Gulf. For example, in family businesses that later grew into international corporations. But also coming from state run enterprises formed by the businesses of ruling families. Many of these top bosses today possess the same key talent of their ancestors: the ability to make decisions. Some of them can even do this incredibly quickly.

CASE STUDY: Decision making power of 21st century Bedouins

This is what international business people say:

> We wanted to build a biochemical lab. The talks were dragging. Although we were already in the last stages of negotiations, we couldn't come to an agreement. On this crucial day, the Arab decision maker was also present. He was a Bedouin and the clan head of his tribe. He listened for a while, without saying anything. At

some point he spoke up, looking me deeply in the eye, and said, "We actually wanted our own people to build this, but now we trust you! So, you should complete the project now!" And that's what happened – we got the contract. – **Werner Piefer, German businessman. Branch: Safety Technology.**

Something to consider: There are similar stories in the government sector in the Gulf, which substantiate the quick decision making power of local top bosses. I'm thinking here of the legendary success story of a famous energy drink manufacturer in the Gulf. The ruling monarch of a Gulf State decided in one meeting, within one day, that from that moment on, this product could be sold in the Gulf State in question. Up to then, it had not been allowed. Or when a former king of Saudi Arabia decided to make the Abdullah Center a reality. As the story goes, the King was playing with a handful of pebbles during the meeting and these inspired the shape of the Center. When he scattered them across the table, they formed a shape that thrilled him. He is reported to have said, "This is what the Center should look like!" Right away a contract was drawn up. These are simply the benefits of a monarchy

But you won't always have the luxury of sitting across from a king or sheikh. There it's perfectly clear who the boss is. But what do you do when the top boss who is also the decision maker does not reveal his identity at the first meeting? Or a whole group attends the meeting? How do you spot the decision maker in a situation like this?

This is what Arab business people say:

You have to find out who in this tribe is still active and the real decision maker. Build up a relationship to this person. Show them respect. Then they will do everything for you! – **Abdullah Kuzkaya, German manager. Branch: Power Engineering.**

How to identify the Arab decision maker in the Gulf: a four-step program

Step 1 – The decision

For this first step you need to ask yourself: "Am I really ready to do everything to get to know the Arab decision maker?" Maybe some answers automatically pop up such as: "How am I supposed to meet these people? It's simply impossible! They're never at our meetings!" Or: "I can't just go above the head of my counterpart and contact the man at the top directly – that's just not possible." If you can only think of arguments for why it can't happen, instead of coming up with constructive suggestions, then I urge you to skip on to the next chapter. Because without an honest inner readiness to do everything in your power to meet the decision maker, it simply won't work. Meeting the decision maker does take effort! And you need a real inner belief in it. (Also see Chapter 3.1, The FITO Technique)

Step 2 – The preparations

This step entails extensive research and using, for example, the Arab Business Club in the Gulf (see Chapter 4.2) where they can get a general view of the decision makers, because everybody knows everybody in the Gulf. Here too there are different techniques. One especially worth mentioning is "**Ask for help.**"

This is what international business people say:

You can occasionally ask, "Who's making the decisions?" I would formulate the question like this: "We've had a number of talks and found solutions. What do you think – who else do we need to bring on board in order to finalize this?" – **Martina Schwarz, Austrian businesswoman. Branch: IT Industry.**

Step 3 – The realization

Here too, there are many options and approaches. Of course, it all depends on your starting position. Let's go over a few situations with case studies and techniques.

Situation 1: You've already researched who the decision maker is, but still don't have personal access to this key person. How do you proceed?

My advice: Start knocking on doors!

Technique: Knocking on doors with the Arab Business Code (ABC)

"Knocking on doors" is a promising technique for new business ties worldwide. And, in different parts of the world, every salesman applies an individual version of it. The successful implementation of this technique with the Arab Business Code requires a special balancing act. On the one hand, you go up to the Arab business person, being almost unpleasantly pushy, something that, at other times in the Gulf, is normally taboo and bad for business. But, in this case, it is done consciously and supports your actions with your inner attitude: "I'm here now! Take note of me!" On the other hand, balance this radical behavior by holding the Arab business person in the highest esteem. Speak to them with the upmost respect. Both these things need to happen at the same time. Only then can you succeed. To better illustrate this balancing act, let me tell you about a case study.

CASE STUDY: *From the secretary to the decision maker*

This is what international business people say:

> I just go there – directly to the office of the top decision maker! I sit down next to his personal assistant. I'm given coffee. I open my computer. "My friend," I say, "Let me show you something." Then I reveal something personal about myself. For example, photos of my last hike, or the new company car. And then he tells a personal story – maybe, about his wife who just threw him out. That he had to spend the night in his car. We joke about it. I tell him I would have frozen my ass off if this had happened in my country, because it's so cold there. Shortly before we collapse with laughter, I ask him: "By the way, does your boss have a minute for me?" He'll reply: "Please wait, I'll just check to see if he's free." Then he knocks on the boss's door and goes in. While he's in there, I can be sure that approaching his boss in such a good mood will definitely help me get an appointment, because the assistant would surely feel extremely bad if he didn't succeed in this. The only reason I might not get to see the boss right away is if he really doesn't have the time. If this is the case, I'll come back. At some point, it'll work out. – **Austrian businessman. Branch: Special Vehicles.**

What you need to know: After all, at some point, the assistants to the top decision makers will become active – and that's when you get the appointment. But you need to invest time and be patient. Another case study about this.

CASE STUDY: *Great patience leads to results*

This is what international business people say:

> After I've researched who the decision maker is, then I sit at his door, even if it takes two or three days. Then I ask: "Where's the general manager?" and say: "I'd like an appointment with him." His personal assistant will reply: "I'll see if he's free today." If I'm

lucky, he'll see me right away. If not, the assistant will tell me: "He's busy," and I won't get in. When the assistant says: "Write him a letter," then I write the decision maker a message and give it to the assistant. He stamps this letter, and I take a copy home with me. And fourteen days later, I come back to the decision maker's office – and maybe there's another personal assistant there. So, I'll tell him about the message I left last time. He might say he doesn't have the letter and can't remember one. Then I'll show him the letter with the stamp. He makes another copy. Either I get an appointment here and now or I write another message. And of course, I ask for it to be stamped again. And make a copy of it. When I've gone through this three or four times, then I have demonstrated such strong interest that the assistant can no longer put me off! And the time will come when I will sit across from the decision maker." – **Werner Piefer, German businessman. Branch: Safety Technology.**

Situation 2: You haven't done the research and can't pick out the Arab decision maker in the group at the negotiating table. How do you proceed? Here is a proven technique.

Technique: Tactical questions with the Arab Business Code (ABC)

CASE STUDY

This is what international business people say:

If, at the first meeting, not all negotiating partners are sitting around the table, it can be very confusing. First three other business partners come in, then five of them leave, and at some point, another two will join you. In a situation like that I can ask calmly, and respectfully, who is responsible for what. I'd put it like this: "Thank you very much for the meeting today. I want to introduce myself – My name is X, I'm the managing director of company Y. We'll do a presentation for you today for Z. And you might introduce yourself as well – so we know who's specialized in what area." Or you say: "It'd be helpful if you could give me a better understanding by introducing yourselves." – **Martina Schwarz, Austrian businesswoman. Branch: IT Industry.**

The Arab Business Code (ABC): You can always ask, if you do it respectfully. It's often the case that the "top people," the true decision makers, tend to be very passive during a meeting. These people, sometimes, don't say a single word the whole meeting. Despite this, they are the ones who are essential for closing the deal. The reason is these people don't want to appear pushy – they know exactly who they are, so they don't need to announce it loudly. The businesswoman in the above case study used a very smart tactic to get the high level people to introduce themselves. Thus, she managed to define the hierarchy structure in just a few minutes. So, none of the counterparts can pose as the decision maker, if they aren't one. It's hardly possible, if they are sitting right next to their boss. Also, within the group, the Arab business people cannot place themselves higher than they are.

And there's another technique that helps identify the Arab decision maker, in a very diplomatic way.

Technique: study the behavior, gestures and facial expressions

CASE STUDY

This is what international business people say:

> *You can immediately see who the decision maker is in a meeting, if everyone keeps looking at him. Very submissively, with great respect. They never interrupt him. Even if he doesn't say anything – then you can tell who the boss is. After the second or third meeting you'll know for sure. He'll be sitting at the front, not in the back. Maybe he won't speak but, if he does, then he'll choose his words carefully. And no one will contradict him. You can tell who's in charge, or who the most respected person is. If he makes a remark, no one will challenge it. But, if I say something, it will certainly be questioned.* – **Austrian businessman. Branch: Construction Industry.**

The Arab Business Code (ABC): Facial expressions and gestures and, above all, the "sign language of the eyes of Arab business people" reveal a lot about their inner attitude.

The following tools are very helpful in identifying the top decision maker. If all the local business people at the meeting suddenly stand up when someone walks in the room and if, as of that moment, people become more nervous and the activity in the room increases, then you can be sure: the local boss is close at hand!

Try this: Once you've established who the decision maker is, listen to him carefully, focus on this person. And don't forget, you need to get his direct contact number.

Conclusion: In the Arab business world, you always phone according to the hierarchy, only the top international businessman will phone the top Arab businessman. And when you speak try to maintain a balance and a respectful attitude.

Step 4 – The follow up work: stay with the top boss!

Staying in contact with the decision maker is probably the most important step of this program because only after you have finally identified him and gotten to know him does the real work begin – like in any relationship.

Often the decision maker will delegate, from the very first meeting, the follow up negotiations to his employees or even his family members. Maybe it's even the son of the decision maker who will be in charge of finalizing the contract. And here's where many international business people veer in the wrong direction. From this moment on they forget to focus on keeping in touch with the "top" decision maker because now they're negotiating with other people who have an obvious say in the matter. This could be, for example, the son of the top decision maker. But this is a serious mistake. The day might come when, at the right moment, you urgently need the "top" decision maker. Let us look at the following case study.

CASE STUDY: *Ask the wise father for advice*

This is what international business people say:

> I was having a communication problem with the son of a government leader, who was running a hotel for his father. He was my direct contact and also my "boss." The time came when the young man stopped listening to me; he didn't agree with any of my suggestions and was very aggressive toward me at meetings. He also didn't offer any constructive suggestions. We had come to a stalemate where there was nothing I could do. But we had to make a decision. That's why I called the father, the owner of the hotel, who I had kept in touch with over the years. I said to him on the phone: "Your Highness, Sheikh, how are you? How is your family?" and then I told him that his hotel was running well, that the occupancy rate was great – with lots of families and children. I reported very

positive things to him, and I squeezed in: "I have a small problem with your son." Then I added: "You know him better than I do, so, I need to ask you for some advice." I told him the whole problem. We said goodbye. The next day I got a call from the son, he had been totally "transformed," was very polite to me and totally cooperative. We agreed on a meeting for the very next day, where we actually did come up with solutions together. And I could continue my work.
– Jean-Pierre Simon. Swiss manager, Branch: Hotel Industry.

What you need to know: In situations like this, you have to react quickly. And that's why there needs to be an intact relationship to the top decision maker. If you are still building up this relationship during the moment of crisis, it will be hard to find a solution. Above all, the level you communicate to the top decision maker on has to be appropriate.

In the case study we just heard, the international businessman applied a special technique – I call it the "Emergency Technique with the Arab Business Code."

Emergency technique with the Arab business code (ABC).

This technique applies a kind of "call for help" to the top decision makers, hence the name. But it's also important to make sure you don't "beg" and, thereby, "lose face." Show the same respect for yourself, because you're only asking politely for advice. This honors the decision maker, because you're conveying the idea that he's the "wise" person in this conversation. Honor and respect, ladies and gentlemen – never forget that in any type of communication you have with the top leaders.

Another clever tactical move in combination with this "emergency technique" is used by the international businessman: he never directly criticizes the son of the top decision maker. Blood is thicker than water, as the saying goes. In the Arab Gulf, this saying is certainly true. Families in the Gulf stick together! That's why you must always speak respectfully to top leaders about their sons. Even if you are boiling with anger.

And that we've mentioned how to manage hierarchies, let us examine hierarchy management with the Arab Business Code in more detail.

Hierarchy management with the Arab Business Code (ABC)

In the Arab Gulf, in the scope of your business activity, you will run into numerous and different constellations, which are determined by diverse family circumstances. Here is an overview of possible constellations and tips and tricks for the right approach to the hierarchies in the Arab Gulf.

The father-son constellation in business cooperation

CASE STUDY: *The cooperative son*

This is what international business people say:

An international businessman had a meeting with the top leader of an Arab family business in the Gulf States and introduced his business idea to him. His goal was a joint project. The son of the decision maker was also present. During the meeting, the top leader officially introduced his son as the decision maker for this endeavor – the father handed over the reins to the son, the "crown prince," allowing him to make the business decisions. He emphasized this, again and again. When the father was absent, at the following meetings, the international businessman took it as a sign that the young Arab businessman was the true final decision maker on this project. They worked out a cooperation contract.

The young man was very cooperative and promised that it would be signed by the end of the month. The deadline passed. The international businessman let another week go by, he didn't want to pressure his partner. He was convinced they would finalize the contract. But when he had still not heard from his Arab partner by the end of the week, he tried to call him. He didn't pick up, nor did he call back. Even after a series of phone texts and messages left with his personal assistant, there was no response. Slowly, the international businessman grew insecure and asked himself: "What just happened?" They had agreed on everything, and the young Arab business man had seemed enthusiastic. What had he done wrong?

What you need to know: Of course, there are sons who can make independent decisions for the Arab family business. But don't always count on that! Basically, the code goes: outwardly, the father lets the son act on his behalf, but the final decision has to be cleared with the father. And this means the father remains the top leader! The family heads hold the business scepter firmly in their hands, which is understandable. Some of them have built up their empire on their own. So, they can't allow anything that might hurt their "baby," namely their "business."

But let's look at this case study more closely – what happened in the meantime? After the young Arab businessman came to an agreement with the international businessman and they were prepared to sign a final contract, the real work began for the son. From then on, he had to negotiate it with his father, he had to convince him of all the points and get his approval. This was also the time to test the son's "sale's pitch," see if it was persuasive enough, if the father took him seriously in a business sense. And what's most important here is: can he reply professionally to all the father's questions, and present the right arguments in favor of the deal?

This seemed not to be the case in the above example. That's why the young Arab businessman didn't get back to the international businessman or respond to his numerous phone calls. He didn't want to lose face. He couldn't reveal that he wasn't the real decision maker. Or, maybe the son was still in the midst of his "negotiations" with his father, and just needed more time to persuade him. That too, was not something he wanted to admit to the international businessman. Perhaps, he just needed stronger arguments that would have helped him to convince his father.

There is also a third possibility, the most fatal one: the father, in the meantime, had reservations about working with the international businessman. And that placed the son in an even more difficult position because, by turning down the project, he would have conveyed his weakness to the international businessman and lost face in the process.

So, what should you do?

Try this: You need to empower the "crown prince," the son, in his sales pitch to his dad. To do this you have to literally "fill him in" on all kinds of information. The son has to be confident in his presentation to his father – so he needs to understand everything, especially if it's a project that's very technical. Only if he really understands the deal, and is thoroughly persuaded by it, can he sell it to his father, in a believable way.

This is what international business people say:

You should invest in this young man, by creating totally new ideas for him which he can present as his own. For example, when he sits down to talk to his family members, when he can tell them about it, and if his father is present. Then he can strengthen his sales pitch to his father. With all these efforts you will ensure long term cooperation with a strong partner, who can help you reach your business goals faster. And also, complete lots of the projects in a short time. – **German businessman. Branch: Food Industry.**

This businessman has the right idea: there's no room here for your own vanity.

Try this: Think of yourself as a coach to the young Arab business partners. Try to see things from their point of view, empathize with them and try to understand their needs. For this you need to forge a relationship together. You have to build trust, so they'll allow you to get closer to them. Only then will you be able to recognize their talents, but also their weaknesses. Once you have identified these, this is where you can start to support them. And when I say support, I mean practical support, like practicing a sales pitch for the locals´ dad. As the businessman above just said, you want a strong partner! That calls for intensive work on the relationship!

The government constellation in business cooperation

In this constellation too, there's a "top leader" who is officially the decision maker. But unofficially the final decision is made by the responsible government department. Here is where the power of group dynamics comes into play. It's best to hear this from a local from the Gulf, who works in the government.

This is what Arab government employees say:

> *For example: I work for the government and have the responsibility and authority to sign a contract for over $80 million. So, I think, "OK, let me just check upstairs." I go to the manager of this department and ask him, "Should I do this?" And the manager will answer, "Let me just check upstairs," and he'll go to the manager of another department and ask as well: "What are your thoughts? Should I do this?" And so it goes, on and on. Although we like to have responsibility and authority it's not always possible to make big decisions on our own, without seeking the opinions or approvals of other departments or our senior managers.*
> – **Government employee from the Gulf.**

This is the culture in the Arab Gulf that is coded by "discussing things with one another until a consensus is reached." The "place of sitting" (*Majlis* or *Diwan*) is especially popular for this. Many final decisions have been made here, because the opinion of the group serves as support. Especially if the business fails, you can always refer back to the approval of the group or, for example, "the place of sitting." This news can be spread and communicated in detail there. Is this kind of behavior bad? No – it's just another culture. And it takes time to get the group's collective opinion. You need to be clear about that and have the right amount of patience.

What you need to know: The official "final decision maker" in the government will only agree once he has the approval of the group and is one hundred per cent certain. So, there's no point in calling all the time and pressuring him! The final decision maker is already working on it – he simply needs time to clear it with his people, "internally." Allow your counterpart this time. The good news is, as long as nothing has been rejected, you're still in the game!

Try this: Come up with a list of measures that entails tactics and questions, on how you can directly influence and speed up a final decision.

Here are some possible questions:

- Who is influencing your project? What departments are these decision makers in? What character traits do they have?
- How is the "hierarchy" set up, what is the individual decision maker's position within the group? Don't forget: the most reserved person can be the most powerful, the one who influences the entire group, and therefore he is the one who makes the final decisions on the project.

Examples of possible ABC tactics:
Here are some goal-oriented tactics, to help the individual decision maker keep you in mind and generate support for the project.

One recommended tactic and something that is also an integral part of the culture is "gift giving." In addition to the choice of gift here, what's also important is how to present the appropriate gift, and in the course of doing so, elegantly inquire at what stage the project is at, or which department it is currently in. You need to find out how to support that department in their decision process. This could be skillfully formulated when addressing the final decision maker, by saying: "I assume you like to exchange opinions and get advice, before you make a final decision. How can I help you with that? How can I support you?"

It's also advantageous to make strategic use of the often mentioned "place of sitting." Here you generate enthusiasm for your project, again and again. You could, for example, mention, "between the lines" that other parties are interested, but naturally you want to realize your project with people from the Gulf States, who you are currently negotiating with. The "exclusivity effect" – the desire to get something that others want – will stimulate the group to make a final decision faster.

But, as I said, you need to practice your "performances" for the "place of sitting." Only then can you achieve the desired success.

Additional important details on hierarchy management in business cooperation.

Your level must always correspond to that of the Arab business partner.

This is what Arab business people say:

> *Usually, when I or my brothers go to meetings, we expect to be received by seniors and owners.* – **Dr. Abdulrahman Alzamil, prominent Saudi Arabian businessman of a big family business, active in diverse areas.**

CASE STUDY: *Loss of acceptance – that's not my level! I won't sit down to a meeting with this man!*

This is what international business people say:

> *A company had a big development in Riyadh. They sent one of their international executives to consult with the Saudi Arabian CEO. After the meeting, the executive did not delegate the work to his colleagues but did everything himself. In the following meetings, the Saudi businessman stopped communicating with him directly, but only through the executives of his own organization. This was a clear sign that the international business executive was no longer hierarchically accepted by the Saudi CEO.* – **Kevin Cushing, American manager. Branch: Information and Communication Technology Services.**

The Arab Business Code (ABC): Business people from the Gulf want to communicate with people on their own level, because it means preserving the hierarchy. Especially in Saudi Arabia, people are historically conditioned to attach great importance to hierarchies, because the country is divided into clans, into tribes. It makes sense that the head of a tribe talk to another head of a tribe – here we are referring, again, to the honor and respect due the "top leader." It appears insulting when an international business person forgets this. As expected, the Saudi in our case study reacted by ignoring the executive. He just wanted to make it clear that: "This is not my level! I will not sit down to a meeting with this man, anymore!"

Always remember: Their rank needs to be the same! It doesn't matter if you send an employee or take part in a meeting with Arab business people or go yourself – your side has to have at least the same rank as the business partner from the Gulf!

And something else is also important to the top leaders in the Gulf. Besides the same rank, they also prefer a counterpart who is a bit older. Older business partners are very welcome in the Gulf.

This is what international business people say:

Especially the Saudis have great respect for "older" senior personalities. That's why companies should send people with experience to Saudi Arabia – the "old hands" not the young inexperienced ones. Because it doesn't go over well. For the Saudis it is almost an insult, as if the company were saying the local was not good enough for them. As if he were not to be taken seriously. – **Abdullah Kuzkaya, German manager. Branch: Power Engineering.**

Written documentation has to be cleared, on a hierarchical basis, with the Arab counterparts – this also goes for business cards!

CASE STUDY: *It would be best if you send your managing director – business card with the "wrong" title*

This is what international business people say:

At first, I had "Area Sales Manager" written on my business card. I never had a problem with it, because I knew my position, knew that I was authorized to make decisions. And the company belonged to my parents. I had a meeting with one of our Arab business partners, a member of the younger generation, who was very direct in the way he acted. We exchanged business cards and started negotiating – hours at a time.

We came to a point where we were no longer in agreement. This is when the businessman said: "Anyway – it would be best if you sent your managing director, so I can continue the discussion with him." I replied: "That's me" and he said, "But it doesn't say that on your business card!" I explained to him that I was the only one in my company who was authorized to sign. He told me: "That's good, but it's not on your business card." I made it very clear that the only person who was above me in the hierarchy was my father, as the owner of the company. My counterpart demanded: "Then bring your father." And he stuck to that. I couldn't prove to him that I could make decisions on my own, in the name of the company, because he kept pointing to the title on my business card.

I went home, changed my business card and brought my father along to the next meeting with the Arab businessman. And then the contract was signed. Without my father, we never would've closed the deal. During the final negotiations, the young business man spoke mainly to my father. – **Martina Schwarz, Austrian businesswoman. Branch: IT Industry.**

The Arab Business Code (ABC): When you design the business card you will leave with the Arab businessman with, keep in mind not just the content, but also the form, color and font, as well as the thickness of the paper. Remember: business cards in the Arab Gulf are more than just contact information – they are an important part of your personal introduction! And they will be passed along in the group, from hand to hand, within the circle of friends and business associates.

Also be careful when you have your business card translated into Arabic. There are some expressions, but also names, that have double meanings when they are translated. Like the short form of Nick for Nicholas. In Arabic it also means "penis" – so make sure you check your translation carefully before you hand it out.

Always appear as a calm and composed decision maker, who is the "top leader."

This is what international business people say:

Who wants to do business with a weak person? That makes you insecure, because maybe he doesn't know what he's doing, doesn't understand how business works. – **German businessman. Branch: Food Industry.**

Even international business people have a hard time with an insecure counterpart – and Arab decision makers in particular. We already discussed the character traits of the "top leaders" at the beginning of this chapter and confirmed how charismatic and sure of their decisions many of them were. You have to be just as confident when you meet with these people – only then can the Arab decision maker trust you. So, watch out how you communicate!

This is what international business people say:

> I've never met such strong characters like those in the Arab Gulf anywhere else, not even in Eastern Europe. When you are sitting together with the top leaders and discussing a problem there is no reason to "aggressively challenge" anyone. Behaving like that will just make the decision maker angrier. And you get wrapped up in a totally senseless discussion. I would never do that. Instead I listen quietly. But I, also, don't say yes to everything either. – **German businessman. Branch: Construction.**

The Arab Business Code (ABC): Preserving the balance between your own self-assured appearance, on the one hand, and still being able to empathize with your counterparts, and support them, on the other, is the essential factor for success in the Arab world. One very important tip, when it comes to balance: don't ever fly into a destructive rage. And above all, watch out for the "Incensed Anger Rascal." First, listen to everything calmly, without committing yourself, or giving a definite yes or no. If it the anger rises in you, apply techniques to deal with the Anger Rascal.

Try this: Visualize this Incensed Anger Rascal who's "racing" around the corner. Make it perfectly clear to yourself that this naughty little creature only wants you to start a fight with the Arab businessman. It wants to get you to tell your counterpart why you are right. In a very aggressive way. But this is something you will simply not let yourself do! Instead listen with great respect to your Arab partner and let him finish his sentence. But don't say yes to everything either, because you need some time to think it over, see if you can even comply with it. If you don't have an answer right then and there, then simply say: "I'll do my best!" Always be clear and set limits! For, as the Austrian psychiatrist Dr. Reinhard Haller explains: "The other person will only take you seriously, and appreciate you, when he realizes that you are a strong, autonomous person. This needs to be demonstrated very clearly, right away. You have to show you have something to offer. This triggers envy in the counterpart, especially if they are a narcissist. But at the same time, it also elicits admiration. And this combination is especially effective!"

What you need to consider as well: When you act like this, make sure it's balanced. An exaggerated know-it-all attitude is just as bad as an extremely servile one, both are counterproductive. Also keep in mind here, the Gas-Shift-Brake technique!

This is what international business people say:

I need to be respectful, but also state clearly what I want. If I approach too carefully then it might seem I have unfavorable conditions, or maybe even that I'm frightened. A little pressure is always good, but not too much, otherwise things won't move forward. It is also a matter of self-respect to insist on one's rights. – **German businessman. Branch: Construction.**

The bottom line is that they have a goal in mind. They'll tell you about it. But if there's something they want, which you don't – just tell them very honestly. That's the trust issue. A lot of people don't like to do this; they're trying to impress someone by saying yes to everything. But that's wrong. Actually, they're happy to hear your opinions because, at the end of the day, all of us are working toward the same goal – to win. – **Dale Karraker, American businessman. Branch: Aerospace, Energy.**

Be authentic – trust yourself to suggest changes.

Demonstrate your decision making power!

An attitude of quick decision making and, above all, the power to express these decisions quickly, will score you lots of points with the top leaders – assuming, of course, that you have the authorization and enjoy the trust of your company. The "license to decide" directly at the negotiating table impresses others and puts you immediately in a higher hierarchical position. Your counterpart has the feeling of being on an equal footing. This will help you get things rolling faster. You might even have a contract ready to sign in a week's time. "Birds of a feather flock together," as the saying goes.

Above all: Be aware from the outset who the decision maker is at the negotiating table and how he conducts the talks, because sometimes you will only hear these casual remarks about the dissatisfaction with the pricing policy on the side; these comments often go by unnoticed. But there is eye contact, and this speaks volumes. This is what it's all about. You need to grasp, in seconds, what the top leader is trying to say to you.

This is what international people say:

If during the negotiations we begin talking about a discount, I need to know, instantly, if I can grant it. Otherwise, I've lost the business. And it's also a surprise to everyone at the table, when I can give the discount right away, without having to call 700 people first. This greatly impresses and wins over the decision maker. – **Austrian businessman. Branch: Construction.**

You have to be prepared to walk away from the table. It's a disaster, but in Saudi your partners gain respect for you if you leave the table. I had that situation. My company authorized me to do so beforehand and I could just tell our partners that I couldn't go any lower with the price. – **Gary Newman, American manager. Branch: Aerospace**

What you need to know: This is also an option – "being able to say no" at the negotiating table. It demonstrates to your counterparts your position in the hierarchy of your company. So, make sure you determine, beforehand, exactly how far your power to decide stretches – explain it to your superiors, how important this point is in negotiations in the Gulf.

Behave according to your position!

CASE STUDY: *The top leaders don't act like coffee boys (service staff)*

This is what international people say:

I remember I was sitting in our office in California with a US senior and a Saudi senior. The US senior asked the Saudi if he'd like to have some tea or coffee, and the Saudi asked for tea. The American got up and went down to the cafeteria himself to get him the tea. I was shocked and looking at the Saudi I saw that his reaction was the same. In his eyes, the American senior communicated a very bad message. – **Dale Karraker, American businessman. Branch: Aerospace, Energy.**

The Arab Business Code (ABC): Especially in the US it's normal, even for managers to get up from their desks, go down to the cafeteria and get their own coffee, tea, or snack and bring it back to their desks. US managers do not pick up the phone and ask someone to bring tea or coffee. That's a question of corporate culture. In Saudi Arabia the office dynamics are totally different. Acting like that conveys the message that the manager is not important enough to talk to, because he's behaving like a coffee boy in the Gulf region.

4.3 GOLDEN RULE NO. 3: RESPECT

It is very important to the Arab businessman that he is respected in everything he does. That's the basic rule. And if you don't follow it, then you won't be taken seriously by Arab business people. – **Saud Al-Arfaj, well-known businessman from Kuwait, active in diverse business areas.**

All communication in the Gulf is based on respect. Whether it be visible (verbal), or invisible (nonverbal). I address it in various chapters in the book. But why is respect so fascinating and important that I have to declare it a golden rule? There are diverse hidden shows of respect that might not be innately obvious to international business people which, if applied correctly, can successfully cement the business relationships in the long run. This allows both sides, international and Arab business people, despite their different cultures, to pull together.

Before I go into detail on these, I need to ask you a few important questions.

Check your personal attitude: am I ready?

First: are you prepared to look at the "hidden shows of respect" in detail? Second: do you want to go along with the "otherness" of your Arab counterparts, while still maintaining your own individuality? Third: do you want both sides to profit from the business cooperation?

You should answer these questions honestly. At the same time, carefully note which arguments and associations this immediately calls to mind. Your response might be something like: "Differences are all good and fine, but now we need to concentrate on the business part of it. Our first priority is earning money, then we can deal with the other aspects. We are not a charity organization. After all, I have invested money in this whole thing. And of course, the partners need to make a profit. But it's *me* who has to benefit first."

If your answers are more filled with "Me" than "We," then ask a further question: does the topic of "shows of respect" cause you to become aggressive inside, because in your opinion, it doesn't really lead to business success in the Gulf, and is an absolute waste of time? If this is your honest answer, then I suggest you skip this chapter, move on, because you are not receptive to this technique. This is exactly what it's all about in the Arab Gulf – you need to become more intuitive. Train your perception more, to pinpoint all of these many small codes of respect early on.

If, however, your answer uses "we" as much as "me," it suggests you are genuinely (from the inside out) interested in joint business success, and I cordially invite you to examine my findings. Under my guidance, you can discover a bit of this valuable "cement" provided by hidden shows of respect.

Key Code 1: Clarity and truth in communication

This is what Arab business people say:

> *When we make a deal – we want to see it! We don't buy fish in the sea! We buy the fish when it's outside the sea!* – **Ahmed Hassan Bilal, prominent Qatari businessman, active in diverse fields of business.**

Tool 1: Be authentic!

"You will know them by their fruits" – as the Bible says (Matthew 7:16). That is very appropriate for people from the Gulf region. They too have grown tired of "nice words." Many things have happened to them in the meantime – they have been lied to, betrayed. Maybe you remember the golf course in Dubai, where the international developer managed to build himself a second golf course in Europe on the same budget. Or the incident where people were injured due to the faulty construction of houses. Or the medical devices that locals bought which exploded in hospitals. When these things happened, Arab business people were held accountable. The international companies had already fled the country. The consequence: the Arab businessman is left behind in his country with a damaged reputation. In his own community. These breaches of trust have spread distrust amongst people in the Gulf. They have become skeptical – and the bad experiences have shaped them. So, let your "deeds," and those of your company, speak louder than your words!

This is what international business people say:

> *Don't speak insincerely with the local! Don't play games or pretend you are someone you aren't or can deliver something you can't. These people have already had plenty of bad experiences.* – **Jürgen Löschenkohl, Austrian manager. Branch: Furnishings, Design.**

This is what Arab business people say:

> *The best thing for me is if I'm invited to see your factory – to see with my own eyes how your company manufactures your product. And to*

see the machines for myself. That's the biggest gift you can give to me!
– Fouad M.T. Alghanim, prominent Kuwaiti businessman from
a big business family, active in diverse fields.

Tool 2: Tell the right story!

CASE STUDY: Ask yourself seriously: "Are we specialized in that?"

This is what Arab business people say:

> *You see, I know this international company – we jointly managed a project for the government over the course of three years. Then the government put the project on hold, so we had to wait. Suddenly, my partner called me and said "Ibrahim, we're getting business in a different line of work!" I told them: "Guys, that's not our branch!" And that's the problem. Many big companies can't say no. They just take and take – even if they are not specialized in the task. And finally, the government loses trust in them. And the companies lose their integrity in the Gulf.* – **Ibrahim Alkindi, well-known businessman from the United Arab Emirates, active in diverse business fields.**

What you need to know: In talks during the signing of the contract, you have to make sure you communicate very clearly exactly what you can and cannot deliver and do precisely what you have promised. Many business people forget to think this through, especially in the beginning when the euphoria is at its peak. Beware of "Insatiable Greed." It is one of the Seven Emotional Hinderers when doing business in the Gulf. Don't let yourself be seduced by this creature. The consequences are brutal, lead to huge problems and a loss of reputation. I know of numerous case studies with very bad outcomes.

Learn to assess your capabilities correctly and don't be afraid to say no. In the long run, it will bring you more business than you ever thought possible. And that brings me to Tool 3:

Tool 3: Learn to say NO with the Arab Business Code, to achieve a YES for new business opportunities

Arab business people respect international companies that know their limits and how to set them. A well-placed "no" – if you simply can't fulfill their wishes – helps you maintain respect and even build up a long-term partnership. Always saying only "yes," will ultimately create problems or cause the project to fail.

CASE STUDY: *A failed billion-dollar project – by just keeping quiet and saying "YES" in the Gulf*

This is what international business people say:

> I remember a planned joint venture by an Emirati company and an international company. Establishing a new company takes time. So, during the building of this company they already took on a huge project. And anyone who understands business, knows running a big project while at the same time establishing a company needs a definite plan. If you do not have a clear-cut strategy, it will not work. You need to make it very clear who's doing what and determine how the organization is run. And if you can't do that, you should say: "I can't do it." But this company kept quiet and just said yes to everything. And they failed after five years. It was a billion dollar project that failed. – **Ibrahim Alkindi, well-known businessman from the United Arab Emirates, active in diverse business fields.**

What you need to know: Here a simple "no" could have prevented the international business failure and the loss of an enormous investment. A "no" can also pave the way to a trust based partnership:

CASE STUDY: *Added value by sticking to deadlines and providing quality*

This is what international business people say:

> You start with the price, give a discount. And if that doesn't help, I say: "This is my limit, I'm not here to give you gifts, but to do business." Then my business counterpart might say something along the lines of: "I can get that cheaper from India or China." So, I say: OK, then get it from India or China. But they won't deliver at 2 p.m., but at 4 p.m. If I say you'll get the delivery by 2 p.m. you will get it by 2 p.m. And if my sticking to deadlines and my quality guarantees are worth it to you, then stay with me. But if you think that's not worth your while, then you have to go with someone else. I can understand that.

After that, I'd get up, say goodbye with respect, and leave. I've done this many times – and sometimes I lose the contract because of it. But then there are times when I get a message confirming our deal the very next day. Followed by a call from the prospective partners saying: "We are happy with you! And we respect this!" I am even complimented on my tough negotiations, and I have often heard how much the partners are looking forward to the cooperation – by the way, which then goes smoothly every time. Incredible! I never thought that was possible!
– **Robert Wiessler, Austrian businessman. Branch: Service and Equipment for Construction Sites.**

The Arab Business Code (ABC): Of course, a "no" in business negotiations can also go the other way. You need to be aware of that – you might actually lose the deal. But one thing you will most certainly not lose is the trust of the locals. And that is the best foundation for them coming back to you with a new project one day. Because, by being able to say a confident "no" you have presented yourself to the Arab businessman as a reliable and equal partner. You are also conveying that he's communicating on par with his equals, on the same hierarchical level. So, this self-assured behavior is a show of respect and builds the corresponding trust for further cooperation.

Another important thing to consider: It's not *what* you say, but *how* you say it! Don't forget that even when you are saying no you still need to be sensitive to the Communication Culture with the Arab Business Code. Don't blurt things out directly and abruptly, but always deliver a respectful reason for everything.

Tool 4: Keep your promises!

This is what international business people say:

> *Then the question is sure to follow: "Don't you want this contract?" To that I reply: "I greatly appreciate your offer. But under these conditions I can't accept it, otherwise I would be lying to you. And I don't intend to make any promises I can't keep!"* – **Kevin Cushing, American manager. Branch: Information and Communication Technology Services.**

Keep in mind, this too is an Arab Business Code, Arab business people have a very extensive and detailed archiving system. Any kind of verbal agreement, even if it only said in passing, will be stored in their memories, to the minutest detail. This archiving system is active 8,760 hours a year! That's why you need to be extremely careful when making any kind of price concession, even if it's only a verbal one!

This is what Arab business people say:

> It's more important to keep one's word than to sign a piece of paper. Maybe in the west you regard written contracts as most important, but here it's "the word." That's what trust is built on." – **Rashed Al Mazrouei, well-known businessman from a big business family of the United Arab Emirates, active in diverse fields of business.**

This is what international business people say:

> Here you need to be cautious, it's not like in Germany or in the west. Here you have to keep all your promises. Especially what you said during the negotiations – there are always issues, where points in the contract pop up that have not been understood. And they have been hastily agreed upon. In Europe that's not a problem, you can always renegotiate or even cancel the contract later. It's normal and okay to do so. But here in the Gulf, this kind of attitude is seen as a breach of trust. And if you withdraw a commitment, it has massive consequences of a business nature. It will be held against you. – **German manager. Branch: Construction.**

> I never say yes to everything – no matter how emotional or tough the discussion is. Because, at that moment, I don't know if I can even fulfill those conditions. You have to watch out, because the Arab business people listen very carefully and remember exactly what you have said. – **German manager. Branch: Food Industry.**

> When you have negotiated a price during the first meeting, then it is very hard to raise this price again. Especially if it's for the same service. That is why you never go down too low. – **Robert Wiessler, Austrian businessman. Branch: Service and Equipment for Construction Sites.**

The Arab Business Code (ABC): Before you agree to something which you are not one hundred per cent sure you can deliver, apply the Gas-Shift-Brake technique. For example, with the words: "I will do my best to get this done." Then look your business partner in the eye and list all the steps you plan to undertake to achieve this, in the near future. Everything that you will actually do. Consequently, you must deliver your promises. Down to the very last detail.

Key Code 2: Use the building blocks of Arab negotiation culture

But what is Arab negotiation culture?

This is what international business people say:

We had a watertight contract – everything was clear. The next day, the Arab businessman called with additional requirements. And again, tried to change a few points. – **Austrian businessman. Branch: Construction.**

Gulf people love to negotiate, oh man! Have you ever been to a souk, an open-air market? They haggle and haggle. If you want to get a good price at a souk the locals from the Gulf will get you the best. They are world masters in that! Learn from them. – **Gary Newman, American manager. Branch: Aerospace.**

This is what Arab business people say:

It's a principle of the past, from the old generations. It's just thinking how to benefit from the negotiation. It's like a game – I win, or you win. It's a challenge. And the bargaining already starts with small things. I get the best product for the best price. That's a real personal achievement for them. – **Dr. Aisha Darwish Alkhemeiri, from the United Arab Emirates, who is active in the health profession. Branch: Medical Care Business.**

What you need to know: Arab business people enjoy continually asking for a price reduction. A business venture is only deemed successful if there's one last price reduction before it's signed. The negotiation ritual is well known: I pay 10,000 – but now I want not five pieces but six. Or, for the 50 pieces, I won't pay 10, but 9. Arab businesspeople are absolute pros in this continuous "counter-arguing." It's a reflex of the Arab Business Code, which shouldn't be taken as a personal affront. By no means should you try to ward off these kinds of negotiation. It would be a complete waste of time and energy. Exactly the opposite is the case: Be smart and learn this technique, so you can use it when you meet the locals. Then you'll have a totally new way of thinking about bargaining with the Arab Business Code, start looking forward to renegotiations! See it as a challenge you must meet and overcome. Be open to this and exercise the special negotiation technique in groups, going over diverse scenarios.

Under the motto: Let the negotiation games in the Gulf begin!

In our coaching seminars we regularly work with different visualization techniques, to help business people see the fun of negotiating. Because if you practice this technique on a regular basis, the "rollercoaster" of ups and downs between small talk and negotiations will get into your blood. As always, it's just a matter of inner attitude.

Try this: Start visualizing your negotiations. Watch yourself and your business partners as if you were sitting in the theater or cinema. Clearly imagine both sides laughing during the negotiations and being in a great mood, engaging in totally relaxed small talk. Then listen to yourself bargain: "I want that; I can't do that; I want this; I can't really do that." Between the haggling you drink coffee with your counterpart and chat about what you did last weekend. And then you go back to bargaining. You'll notice, inside you, that the haggling is beginning to be more and more fun, that you're slowly but surely becoming a pro at bargaining, by using the Arab Business Code. Along with good preparation and your newly won "joy of bargaining," further building blocks will help support a strong foundation for your concrete negotiations in the Arab Gulf.

Building block 1: before the negotiations – establish a clear starting position

What you need to know: Who are you – and who are the others? You need to be totally sure of this, before you step into your first meeting. We addressed this in chapter 1.3. ("Your Professional Competence"). You must be completely aware of your strengths and weaknesses, especially your selling power. And then you'll have the self-confidence to stage really good talks with your negotiation partner.

Building block 2: during the negotiations: use the Arab Business Code (ABC)

Let's go over the classic negotiation and communication with the Arab Business Code. Let the case studies sink in and internalize which codes you expect from your counterpart. With a little practice and the right attitude, you can apply this yourself. Precisely when and where it suits you best.

Code 1: Recognize the value of the time investment

Allow yourself enough time for your talk and also imagine the waiting period. Stressed out behavior does not go over well with Arab business people; it's seen as a total insult. Because if you're generous with your valuable time, you not only show interest, but also respect.

CASE STUDY: *Patience is rewarded*

This is what international business people say:

I go to the negotiations with a very specific attitude – I don't have any expectations, no special time pressure or time schedule. When it comes to important meetings, then I take the time; there's no limit for this. Because first of all I need to see what kind of mood my Arab counterpart is in on that particular day. Then the small talk starts: "How are the kids? How's the family?" This kind of behavior goes over well, pleases my counterpart, especially in the beginning. And before we say goodbye – without me having once mentioned business – he says on his own: "In two months, we'll have the project. Then we'd like to work with you and make you an offer!"
– Austrian businessman. Branch: Construction.

Just do nothing and see what happens – it will give you the chance to let the person opposite you act. He could do or say something. In this way, you can adjust to your counterpart's behavior and place yourself in a very calm and stable starting position. This is excellent for further negotiations. **– Martina Schwarz, Austrian business-woman, Branch: IT Industry.**

They have plenty of time! Negotiations can last five hours. As an international business person, you need to have that time available. If you come to a meeting and say, from the beginning on, that you only have ten minutes, then your Arab partner is more than likely to walk out for half an hour to get something else done. That's why you need to be flexible with your time. And there is just one thing you need to keep in mind: I'm here today to do business! That's why I'll wait. **– Robert Wiessler, Austrian businessman. Branch: Service and Equipment for Construction Sites.**

Try this: Don't schedule too many meetings for the same day. Even two to three meetings in one day can be a problem. Remember that the Arab Gulf, like other business hubs worldwide, has a growing flow of traffic. So, you need to allow for lots of time to get to and from meetings. That's why I suggest one meeting in the morning, and one in the afternoon – that's plenty. And if you can get through these two appointments then you're doing great.

Code 2: Recognize the power of self-confidence – know your worth!

It goes without saying that the basis for building trust is being genuine. Have a confident manner; this is especially important as the negotiations proceed and you start to discuss price. We've often emphasized how important it is to know your final price. And you have to stick to this price, otherwise you will seem untrustworthy.

CASE STUDY: *More is simply not possible!*

This is what international business people say:

Once I was in these negotiations where we kept circling, again and again, around a price reduction. I said: "I only work for my company – and I've reached my limits!" Then the other side argued: "Then we'll go to the board." I replied: "That won't change a thing, because I've already pushed the boundaries. More is simply not possible!" While I said this, I packed up my stuff but didn't stand up yet, and continued speaking: "And how are things going for you?" I asked this as an aside. My ease took my negotiation partner by surprise, threw him off balance, because a lot was happening on a nonverbal level. It's all about the tactic of leaving things unsaid, but letting my counterpart clearly sense what the message is. It was as if I was telling him: "It's not a problem. This time it just isn't working. We'll do business next time." I noticed he was getting nervous. In situations like this it's very rare for negotiations to stop. Because if you have thoroughly convinced the local partner that the limits have been reached, and that you've done everything in your power, then it should work. Then he's sure. And finally, you can reach your desired goal. – **Austrian businessman. Branch: Construction.**

When you go into the next round of negotiations and the Arab businessman starts demanding a better price again, then I say to him: "If you think I can give you a 60% discount then I must have cheated you from the very beginning. That's simply not possible!" And then we make the deal. – **Robert Wiessler, Austrian businessman. Branch: Service and Equipment for Construction Sites.**

Try this: Instead of a price reduction, give your potential partner another kind of "gift." Gifts don't have to be of a material nature. In choosing a gift, think about what would make your partner happy, and come up with a gift list. For this it's essential to have detailed information about your counterpart and his hobbies and passions.

Code 3: Set boundaries with the help of the "third man"

Letting a third person make the decision, even if they don't actually exist, is another successful negotiation strategy in the Gulf. The trick is to not be the one to say no. And in this way, you are maintaining the respect in the communication. Because the one who's rejecting the offer is "the company" or "Mr. X" who's high up in the hierarchy and not you, the negotiator, who is always doing his best for the partner. Again, as often in the Gulf, a lot of time and patience is needed here. And also knowing where to set one's own limits.

CASE STUDY: *Not approved by the "third man"*

This is what international business people say:

> *If you can't agree on a price with your Arab counterpart, you often hear remarks like: "But this is the way we do things." And I reply: "And my way of doing things is that I can't sign a contract with this price and under these conditions!" Then a few sentences later, I say: "OK, I'll ask again and call you tomorrow." Then I think it over calmly and try to see what I can do. Only after I have gone over everything, to the last detail, and am certain that nothing more can be done, do I write my negotiation partner an email. The text is: "I'm sorry, unfortunately it was not approved. But I recommend we go ahead with what I suggested last time." This often works and we go through with the deal.* – **Robert Wiessler, Austrian businessman. Branch: Service and Equipment for Construction Sites.**

What you need to know: Get yourself into the position of postponing a meeting – with the help of the "third man" or "third woman" because it's a powerful argument, saying changes need to be cleared internally first. In this way, you're treating yourself to a pause for thought, and at the same time presenting your counterpart with "an equally strong negotiation partner." It's as if you're saying to yourself: "Let's take a break." You're asking, diplomatically, for a moment to reflect, and aren't losing business through this. Remember: Arab business people love the game of bargaining!

Code 4: Always have balanced negotiations

Even if you were sure the end price had been reached, renegotiations are the order of the day in the Gulf. The "give-and-take" always needs to be kept in balance. When you "give" your Arab business partner something, for example, a further price reduction, the scale is tipped. In this situation you can demand something in return, "take" something from him. This is how things stay balanced.

This is what international business people say:

It's in their DNA to negotiate. Even if they ask for things that are incredibly easy for you to fulfill, don't just answer: "OK, for sure! I'll get you that compensation – let's have that written down in our contract." That answer won't work, you can't do that. You always have to ask for something in return. It's quid pro quo. Because if you don't do that, they'll keep asking for more until you say No! And then they'll think: "What else can I get until he says what he needs from me in return." – **Dale Karraker, American businessman. Branch: Aerospace, Energy.**

What you need to know: Arab business people from the Gulf use the technique of "counterbalance" for one reason in particular: they want to be convinced they've gotten the best possible price. This they can easily find out in the "back-and-forth Q&A" because, at some point, they'll notice if the international business person can go lower, or if they've really reached an end.

A three-point program is effective for this:

1. Go over scenarios, beforehand, about what you're prepared to give up, but also what you'd like in return.
2. Ask two very concrete questions in the renegotiations: "What exactly do you want?" and: "What do you hope to reach through this?" Listen carefully and take it a step further by asking how your counterpart is prepared to compensate you for this.
3. I can't stress this enough – make sure you know, ahead of time, what your final price is. Even better: have several final prices! Then you'll still have "enough room" to keep the negotiations in sync.

Building block 3: After the negotiations – you need to have a clear exit strategy

"Have the end in mind from the start" – this is something the successful Austrian businessman, Senator Professor Rudolf Öhlinger, often said to me. And he was right. You should have an idea, already during the "good times" when everything is running smoothly, about how to behave in case of a "breakup" – if the negotiation or the joint venture fails.

This is what international business people say:

This is something we've learned – to make clear decisions. It can happen that we don't accept the contract, because it has specific liability clauses, which we cannot take over. Then we make the decision – up to this point and no further. – **Jürgen Laky, Austrian manager. Branch: Design of Building Envelopes.**

What you need to know: Rash liability clauses have led to the ruin of international companies in the Arab Gulf. Because, in the euphoria of the start of the business relationship, this is not something one always considers. At this point, the mood, on both sides, is great and people are convinced that everything will turn out fine. But never forget, here two totally different worlds "clash" together. That's why you need to be very clear about your exit strategy. If you don't take this into account, you'll not only lose your investment but also your reputation. And the respect of business people in the Gulf. Failing in one business venture can ruin your chances of successful long-term cooperation in the region.

Key Code 3: Long term commitment and patience

This is what Arab business people say:

This is not a relationship of one or two projects, this is long term relationship. – **Dr. Abdulrahman Alzamil, prominent Saudi Arabian businessman of a large, global family enterprise, active in diverse areas.**

A long-term commitment is the necessary foundation in every kind of relationship, especially for successful business partnerships in the Gulf region. If a partner really trusts you and you have a fruitful business relationship, then this success story will most certainly lead to further deals among the big family and in the partner's social circles.

CASE STUDY: *Trust instead of price policies*

It took me about three months to get to know my Arab counterpart who was supposed to "sell" me to his top people. I provided him with a lot of answers, gave him suggestions, and discussed matters thoroughly, on a private and professional level. Then came the moment he said: "OK, I'm convinced you can do it – I trust you. Next week, I'll arrange for a meeting with one of the twelve generals who heads the military in Abu Dhabi. The meeting will last between fifteen and thirty minutes. This is your chance." I presented my ten minute short pitch to the general, an accomplished, self-controlled man with a stern look. When I finished, he got up and left the room. I looked at my counterpart, and he nodded to me. But still, I had a very bad feeling, and kept wondering what I could've done better. But my Arab counterpart said: "It was fine! You'll get the deal!" I objected that he hadn't even asked about the price. But the Arab businessman replied: "It's not about that. It's just to see if he can trust you or not. And we trust you to do it." And he was right, I got the deal. – **Jürgen Löschenkohl, Austrian manager. Branch: Furnishing and Design.**

What you need to know: The group dynamics in the Gulf should not be underestimated. If, in taking the first step, you've been able to convince the individual Arab businessman, he'll check your background and tell people in his wide personal and business network about you. Ultimately, he'll persuade the whole group that you are right for the job. This is also a great example of the FITO technique, which implies that long term success always has to come from "within" and is always the basis of lasting trust.

But how does one, as an international business person, succeed in establishing this long-term trust? It sounds simple. Be there, at the location, invest time, be patient and don't give up. Here too, you must keep your "boat" from tipping; and don't "capsize." So, let's look at some strategic approaches in building successful business ties with Arab partners. Let's look at how to navigate "your boat" successfully; here are some strategic approaches.

Strategic code 1: Be seen – make your presence known in the Gulf

An international businessman had a meeting with a Saudi businessman in Riyadh, presented his project and offered to work together. The Saudi listened and said: "I'd love to continue our discussion next week. Can we meet in your office in Riyadh?" The international businessman seemed a little bit confused and answered: "Oh no, we don't have an office here. We're living in a hotel in Riyadh." Then the Saudi businessman continued: "But you said you're establishing your presence here, right?"

The international businessman nodded and replied: "Yes, we're working on it." Then the local said: "OK, then please be so kind and come and see me when you actually have a presence here." – **Kevin Cushing, American manager. Branch: Information and Communication Technology Service.**

What you need to know: This is a totally typical situation that keeps repeating itself in the Gulf. International business people want to conduct business from their own countries. The Saudis especially are particularly "allergic" to this. It's seen as pure lack of respect and demonstrates that one wants to earn money in their country but not spend a moment longer there than absolutely necessary.

CASE STUDY: *Back in Dubai – for a drink*

This is what international business people say:

> *A big international company didn't have its headquarters in Riyadh, but in the United Arab Emirates, in Dubai. The company only worked through a distributor in Saudi Arabia, even though it was representing four big companies in Saudi Arabia. At the same time, they were working on a large contract with the Saudis. The representative, who worked as distributor in Saudi Arabia did his job, but never built up a close relationship with his Saudi business partners. As soon as the talks were over, he flew back the same day to Dubai, to spend his weekend there; to have a drink in the local bars. Then the day came when the project was supposed to be handed over, and the Saudis didn't agree to it. They claimed compensation from the company for failing to stick to the contract. The company was showered with financial penalties, followed by court cases. This cost them millions in fines and financial compensation. –* **Werner Piefer, German businessman. Branch: Security Technologies.**

How did this terrible situation come about? The root of the problem was the wrong approach by the international company. They thought themselves to be the strong partner the Saudis needed. The manager assumed it was enough to only travel to the neighboring country for the meetings.

But, unfortunately, this is not the way things work in the Gulf. Even though people from the Gulf States might stick together and be related, still each Gulf State has its very own and personal national pride. This entails locals showing their international partners their country; maybe going on a few trips to the desserts or visiting their family homes, or farms. We already addressed this in Chapter 4.1 on "Chemistry" – "the code" to build up interpersonal closeness. Only in this way can trust come about – even in business cooperation.

This is what international business people say:

It's all about reaching out to your customer, again and again – being open to them. That's why you need to be permanently on site: ready to meet with your business partner or customers, even if it's ten at night, or ten in the morning. The meetings don't have to be about big things. Sometimes it's just a few simple questions, or small stuff. But the permanent presence on the spot, is a display of commitment and trust. Especially in Saudi Arabia, the local presence is very, very important. There was once this German company that offered great high tech, but they wanted to conduct all the business from Germany. And that didn't work. They failed. High tech itself is not enough. You also need to be "highly in touch." – **Abdullah Kuzkaya, German manager. Branch: Power Engineering.**

That is what Arab business people say:

The problem with many European companies is that you can't find them in Saudi Arabia. They are simply not here. But it's essential to be present, to be able to catch up any time, to sit with them in their showroom or office, to talk to them if there's a need. Especially for maintenance, that's very important! – **Saudi Arabian businessman. Branch: Food Industry.**

If you want to do business with me, you need to come and see what I'm doing. You can't come in person just once and then rely on email and the dispatch of your products. Face to face communication is crucial and you need to see what's happening here. – **Omani businessman, active in diverse areas.**

I always say, the player is not like the spectator. And we are the players. Come and sit with the players to learn more. Don't sit in your country and price things in Kuwait. Sit with us, the locals, and discuss why some companies are cheaper although they're using the same products. We have the knowledge – so just sit with us and learn more about this place. – **Fouad M.T. Alghanim, prominent Kuwaiti businessman, of a large family enterprise active in many business areas.**

Here too the message is loud and clear: Arab business people need their partners to be on the spot so they can solve problems at a moment's notice. Because business in the Gulf never stops and the competition is great. That's why people have to act fast together, so that they can build up successful strategies. People in the Gulf need the security of a loyal partner at their side. Always remember this: many Arab business people have had bad experiences with international business people in the past. A lot was promised to them, but in the end, they were delivered equipment and products they couldn't use, or that needed a service that was not available in the Gulf. Left behind were local businessman, having to rely totally on themselves, in their own country. Of course, they felt let down. Therefore, people from the Gulf expect a commitment. And one expression of this is a business presence in the country. Especially in Saudi Arabia this is a must.

Without a doubt, being permanently on location in the Gulf demands the necessary financial backup. That's why you need to decide from the beginning if you can afford a long term stay in the Gulf; if you want to proceed. Because a short visit is not going to work.

Strategic code 2: Practice in "being patient"

If you look at various business cultures worldwide, you will realize that the concept of "getting things done fast" is the main focus. I like to compare it to a kind of checklist, that needs to be gone through quickly.

The Arab Gulf operates in a different way. Here too projects are completed step by step, but in a different tempo, more slowly and carefully. For the international company this behavior means exercising great patience, because the concept of "take it or leave it" will certainly not work for the market here.

That is what Arab business people say:

> *Is this a problem? No, it's just our culture. Everything takes time, and you need to give us the time we need. Stressed executives, who apologize daily with, "Sorry, I need to know now" are not the right way to go. But don't worry, we are working on it. So just give us some time.* – **Businessman from the United Arab Emirates, active in diverse areas.**

Here's the good news: as long as your potential partner has not declined your offer, you are still "in the game." So just practice patience!

Patience management in the first meeting:

CASE STUDY: *Crashing into it – with a sales pitch*

This is what international business people say:

> *I attended a meeting with another international businessman, a banker, and an Arab businessman. Right away, after the greeting, the banker said to the local: "Do you want to get credit with us?" The international businessman stopped him and whispered in his ear: "The guy barely knows your name." The Arab businessman continued talking respectfully with the banker. After some time, he politely said goodbye and arranged for a follow up meeting with me and the international businessman. But not with the banker. He didn't even give him his business card.* – **German businessman. Branch: Food Industry.**

What you need to know: This direct and hasty way of immediately getting to the point is the wrong "code" for the Arab mentality. It clearly and explicitly shows that the international businessman is just interested in a fast deal. That, in the eyes of the local business people, is disrespectful behavior. No wonder that in the above case study no business ties were made.

Try this: Get a sense of what your counterpart is thinking, especially if you're taken to a meeting and still haven't met the Arab partner. Here you need to put in more effort and present your professional background, because your counterpart hasn't had the opportunity yet to "form a picture" of you and do a background check. Act calmly and be patient. When the time is right, present your offer. But always within the Communication Culture of the Arab Business Code.

This is what international business people say:

> *If you're not patient or prepared to invest the time, don't even set foot in the Arab market, you'll be exhausted. A year is no time at all to understand the country and to get to know the decision makers. To get a feel who to talk to – who the people are who really get things done. That takes time.* – **Austrian businessman. Branch: Special Vehicles.**

That is what Arab business people say:

> *You can't just come in as an international company and say: "I have a big name in Europe." Sorry, it takes time for us to get to know and trust you!*

You need to be here for a longer period and understand the culture. And in this time, we, the locals, will learn to understand you as well. – **Businessman of the United Arab Emirates, active in diverse areas.**

You need a little patience! Some western people are sometimes too aggressive. They give you a call, out of the blue, and offer you something. They ask you to buy one of their companies. They want the deal done; they push it on the telephone. They show quiet aggression. That turns me off. – **Omani businessman. Branch: Investments, Hotel Industry, Mining, Gas and Oil Industry.**

If a sales person comes and talks all the time about their company and puts pressure on you to buy – that's not good. It shows that he only wants to sell and not to build a relationship. But a relationship is very important to build trust. So, you need to be patient. – **Salah H. Sobghan, well-known Saudi Arabian businessman. Branch: Food Industry.**

Patience management in the follow up talks

CASE STUDY: *The final talk – "Why are we meeting?"*

This is what international business people say:

I had lots of briefings with the Arab manager of an organization. The young man was new in this position. The talks went very well. We had reached a point where we could agree to a final session and define the terms of the contract. I came to his office. When I sat down, his first question was: "Why are we meeting today? Why are you here?" I was completely surprised but did not let him see this and started with a short summery of our last meeting, very respectfully and without any sort of aggression. Because I knew, today anything can happen; also, that nothing may be decided and I'd need to come back again. – **German businessman. Branch: Construction.**

What you need to know: This businessman is very experienced in the business culture in the Arab Gulf. He's an excellent manager of his expectations and successfully applies the Gas-Shift-Brake technique. He doesn't insist on rushing through his topic but deals respectfully with the questions of his Arab counterparts. Without a doubt, he has a "helicopter view" (an overview of his own actions) and understands that there might be many reasons for his partner's reaction. Maybe the young man is overwhelmed by his new position? Maybe he doesn't even have the power to make a decision on this project and needs to get the approval of his superiors in the hierarchy. Maybe that's the reason he's stalling for time. Or he has a totally different strategy and is asking these questions because he wants to have the complete project presented to him again. Maybe he just wants to hear how convinced the international businessman actually is of the success of his project and if there have been any new developments in the meantime. In short, there are many reasons for this man's reaction and to find these out you have to do something first: be patient and listen carefully!

CASE STUDY: *Keep going – prove you can persevere*

This is what international business people say:

> *These are the unforgettable moments. Once we arranged an evening meeting with a Saudi business man at 11 p.m. at his house. The whole company from Germany came especially to Saudi Arabia for this meeting. As we stood in front of his door, he asked us: "What are you doing here?" And we answered: "We want to talk to you." And he replied: "But we already talked over everything." Either he was tired or he had scheduled something else in the meantime. It didn't matter, I stayed calm; getting angry would only have made matters worse. It would have destroyed the contact between us.* – **Werner Piefer, German businessman. Branch: Safety Technology.**

This is what sets successful entrepreneurs in the Gulf apart – their resolve and tenacity, not losing their self-control even in provocative situations.

If something like this should happen to you, try to keep a cool head – take a sip of water and don't let yourself be manipulated by the "Incensed Anger Rascal" in you, who's shouting: "Who does he think he is? How dare he! Is he crazy? We arranged this meeting, is he making fun of me now?" In this moment, tell yourself, very deliberately: "No! Thank you! I won't let myself be provoked! I'll remain respectful, because I don't want to be maneuvered into a bad starting position! In the worst case, I'll just come back; what difference does it make? I want this deal to work out. That's the most important thing." So, send the Incensed Anger Rascal away, or just tell this hinderer to "relax."

Tell the Incensed Anger Rascal – cool down,
relax!

Patience management when it comes to payment

This is what international business people say:

Even if you're urgently waiting for the payment – it's no use bringing this up directly, after the greeting, at the next meeting, by saying to the Arab businessman: "When will I get my money?" That's not a good strategy. And it's very dangerous. You must have stamina and be able to afford to be patient. Otherwise it just won't work. – **Jürgen Löschenkohl, Austrian manager. Branch: Furnishing and Design.**

What you need to know: Don't shut the door! Always be open for further talks and use the time to develop strategies that could speed up payments. One successful technique is creating the right "vibe" for payment situations, for example, with a "third party" or people who are close to your business partner. Or you can go to the "place of sitting" to a *Majlis*, or the *Diwan*.

There are many other ways: I remember an international business woman who spent months sitting in front of the private office of a top Arab businessman from the Gulf, because he owed her money. It was a high sum, and the woman did not give up; she was there every day. Eventually, the Arab businessman understood the power of her persistence, and was impressed by it. So, she got an appointment and afterward her money. She even went on to work with this man again because she respected an important basic rule: she didn't cause him "to lose face" but cleared up the outstanding accounts directly with him – face to face. And this is the relevant point: this woman didn't talk about the debt with other people – she never uttered a word about it. She just sat outside the door of the Arab businessman asking for an appointment. Every single day.

Patience management in decision making

This is what international business people say:

We had numerous meetings and we, the international partners, had reached a point where we felt all the parties were now ready to sign the contract; so, we sent our partners the contract. But then, from this moment on, we didn't hear anything from them. – **German businessman. Branch: Automobile Industry.**

At the risk of repeating myself: Arab businessman simply need time to agree on a decision. The fear of failure and "losing face" is too great for the person, especially in front of the whole community in the Gulf. So how does one support these people in their decision making?

This is what Arab business people say:

Set deadlines. Write at the end of your offer: "This proposal is valid for x dollars and for two months." If you don't get feedback by then, you start negotiations with a different partner. It's that simple, it's a business transaction. And Arab business people understand that. – **Businessman from the United Arab Emirates, active in diverse areas.**

It's interesting how clear Arab business people, on their part, are about setting limits. Especially with the younger generation in the Gulf, you can see how much they've adopted from the international business culture; they've created a new form of business cooperation from the "old traditions" and the "new" ways.

Strategic code 3: Accept a new definition of time management

CASE STUDY: *"I'm really sorry. I forgot the appointment."*

This is what international business people say:

We had scheduled an appointment with a businessman from the Gulf; we were waiting in his office. An hour went by before he called, and apologized by saying: "I'm sorry, I forgot!" We remained polite, and he gave us a new appointment. And this one he managed to keep. – **German businessman. Branch: Construction.**

What you need to know: The focus is always on the project and its value; you have to decide for yourself exactly how important this deal is to you. If it's very important then you need to be ready to exercise patience, because there is a general principle in the Gulf: many Arab business people have a totally different way of managing time. Time is perceived in another way. The emphasis lies on "many" and not "all" of the people, because, timewise, many people in the Gulf have adapted to the international business culture. They've become much more punctual. I even know Arab businessmen who won't give international business people another meeting, if they don't appear exactly at the scheduled time.

That is what Arab business people say:

If you are fifteen minutes late without any excuse or call – without any reason, then I will not see you again. Being on time is a sign of respect. – **Fouad M.T. Alghanim, prominent Kuwaiti businessman, of a large family enterprise active in many business areas.**

Maybe because I've worked with British people my whole life, I've been trained in time management. I'm always on time, I don't let others wait for me. It's not good to be late! People have invested time in you. And if I give you an appointment and you don't show up on time, I won't see you again. – **Sherida Saad Jubran Al-Kaabi, well-known businessman from Qatar, active in diverse sectors.**

It doesn't speak well for you if you're late! People shouldn't have to wait for you, nor you for them! We should treat people the same! They all have the same feelings! Being late shows you're unprofessional and have the wrong attitude! – **Sheikh Nahayan Mabarak Al-Nahayan, member of the Abu Dhabi ruling family, and a businessman active in diverse areas.**

Another case study on this: I remember an event in the Gulf, in the United Arab Emirates, that started at ten in the morning. All the guests were there, and so was the sheikh. Who wasn't there were the invited international business people. They came late. I don't have to point out that this was a very bad starting point for negotiations, because the locals had lost respect for this company. By now, Arab business people too have understood that punctuality in many cultures worldwide is highly important and being on time earns a high level of respect.

My conclusion: Even if you had to wait for hours at previous meetings – never be late! That rule applies to you – always be on time!

But what can you do if you have to wait for the Arab business partner, and even his secretary doesn't know when he'll come in?

An Arab businessman suggests the following course of action:

Today the culture in the city is different, there's a lot of traffic. Therefore, it's a little bit out of your control whether you're on time or not. It can happen that you have to wait! I'd wait around thirty minutes and then call my partner directly on his mobile phone. I'd ask him in a very polite and friendly way: "How are you? I'm sitting in your office – are you on your way?" And if he doesn't pick up, I'd send him a text message. – **Businessman of the United Arab Emirates, member of a large business family. Branch: Luxury Goods, Hospitality Industry.**

You have to learn to evaluate the situation for yourself, case by case, whether to wait an hour or half a day; it all depends on how important the appointment is for you and if you have other appointments that day. What really matters is: you need to be patient! And never be disrespectful.

Strategic code 4: Invest in building the relationship

"Sharing is caring" – spending time together, exchanging information and thereby gaining trust – this is a worldwide practice and, in the Gulf, definitely. In previous chapters we talked about how relationship oriented this society is. It's not uncommon for deals in the millions to be closed in the desert, by chatting over Arabic coffee. Therefore, invest the time to get to know your partner better. Meet him or her outside of the general business settings. Keep in mind: Small talk and the exchange of personal stories and experiences are not a waste of time, but an essential "lubricant" for the smooth running of successful business. Private get togethers help you gain better insights into the culture and local ways of thinking, to develop empathy and understanding.

Thus, you'll also learn more about the daily problems and challenges your partners face in your work together. And maybe you'll get the chance to pinpoint the perfect solutions.

This is what international business people say:

We invest a lot in the social aspects with our partners: The locals visit us, and we go to the New York Stock Exchange. Or we give them a tour of our projects, have dinner together. This hospitality always works both ways – we also spend time in the desert with them. Or we visit them at their place. And sitting there, chatting with them, you're apt to get more business in thirty minutes than in hours of meetings. **– American businessman, who is active in different business fields.**

That is what Arab business people say:

You need to sit with us. Because we want to guide you as partners in business. Local customers have totally different taste than customers from the rest of the world. So, you need to see and to know the country. **– Abdulrahim Hassan Naqi from Bahrain, prominent figure in the business world in the Gulf, active in diverse areas of business.**

What you need to know: It's always about the same thing – wanting to get to know the Arab partner better. And to gain his trust. If you get the opportunity, and receive an invitation, by all means accept it. And it works the other way around as well – you can also offer an invitation to your Arab partner. Show him your "world" and how much you respect and value him.

Strategic code 5: Never give up!

CASE STUDY: *Finally closing the deal – with tenacity*

This is what international business people say:

We were negotiating with an Arab businessman and everything seemed perfect. My colleague was also convinced that everything looked good – but I had the feeling that something wasn't quite right. Even though he argued I was reading too much into it, I still asked the Arab businessman a direct question: "Can it be that you've already signed a contract with our competitor?" although we had never spoken of competitors before. And I didn't even know if there were any – but I sensed there was something more in the air, so I just put it out there. He looked at me, totally surprised: "How did you know?" I kept on asking questions: "If you don't mind, I'd like to know who it is? And most of all, why?" I wanted to know if it was because of our price, or if there were other reasons behind it – you want to keep on learning! The local didn't respond to my question and changed the subject. By chance, a week later I was passing the house of this Arab businessman and thought I'd drop in. While we were talking, he said to me: "To be honest with you, we're not going to change the contract." That was clear to me; the local then asked why I was here. I replied: "From now on, I need to make sure to give you the feeling and certainty that the next deal will go better with us. And I can't start to do that in ten or five years, I need to do it now." The local continued explaining that he didn't need another car for the next four years. But I answered: "That's great, I have four years' time." A year later, I got a call from this very same local businessman asking if we wanted to sell him some cars. What had happened? His previous supplier couldn't deliver the prototype as agreed. So, he cancelled the contract. – **Austrian businessman. Branch: Special Vehicles.**

This is one of my favorite case studies, because it so clearly proves that there's always a chance of doing business together – but only if you're patient, hang on, stay on the ball, keep at it and don't give up too soon, like this businessman, who managed to ensure a long term relationship, and therefore deserves great recognition and applause. He used all the necessary tools of Arab communication: he showed respect, listened carefully, read between the lines and asked the right questions. And he also applied the Gas-Shift-Brake technique, proving this story can have a happy ending!

That is what Arab business people say:

If you want to do business in Saudi Arabia, in the beginning, it's not easy. But after some time, you will get used to the business environment, and you will have good continuous profits. There are many examples of successful foreign companies who have done it. – **Mohammed Alkhalil, prominent Saudi Arabian businessman, who is active in diverse business sectors.**

Whatever you do that has good quality, even though it might cost you more at first, will pay off in the end. Giving nothing is worthless, giving it one's all is worthwhile! – **Ahmad Almutlaq, well-known businessman from Saudi Arabia, who is active in diverse areas.**

There's another thing in this chapter we need to go over, because it'll help further "cement" all these tiny pieces of the "show of respect" among Arab business people in the Gulf. I call it "Three cultural no-goes of the Arab Business Code." Let's deal with this now in my Key Code 4.

Key Code 4: Three cultural no-goes of the Arab Business Code (ABC)

This is what Arab business people say:

Before you come to any country you need to educate yourself about the culture. Here, in the Gulf, it's the same. But a lot of foreign companies don't realize the mistakes they make. Maybe they don't have bad intentions, but it's still not good and shows me that they don't respect me. Without respect I will not work with you. No matter how much money you offer me. I don't care. It simply won't work. – **Mohamed Jassim Al Rais, well-known businessman of the United Arab Emirates. Branch: Travel Industry.**

What you need to know: Not knowing the cultural no-goes is also a kind of "business blocker" that is not only a bad basis for negotiations, but, in the worst case, can lead to the collapse of the business deal. Let me introduce to you three of these cultural no-goes of the Arab Business Code (ABC).

Cultural no-go ABC 1: soles of the feet

For us, when you show us the sole of your shoe, it's like an insult – you're looking down on me! It shows me that this man doesn't respect me. That it's not worth spending time with him. – **Dr. Abdulrahman Alzamil, prominent businessman of a large Saudi Arabian business family, active in diverse areas.**

This is what Arab business people say:

Once a local partner, a very good friend of mine, brought an international businessman who wanted to cooperate with me. When I entered the meeting room, I spotted the man from abroad, sitting there, waiting for me. And the first thing I saw was his shoe sole. So, I said to myself: I'll talk with him for five minutes, then I'll tell him I have another appointment and let my people continue the meeting. I made it through the beginning of the meeting. But after he said everything, I left. Later on, I said to the local, "You're my friend, but I won't deal with him." He asked, "Why, what did he do wrong?" "He didn't respect me," I replied, and I told him that, at the beginning of our meeting, he showed me the bottom of his shoe. Even if I were the chauffer, I wouldn't accept this type of behavior. It's not a matter of my position – it's about respecting a human being. And believe me, it doesn't matter if it's a CEO, a secretary, or a merchant – I treat them all the same. My friend said, "But he didn't know," and I said, "He should have known!" – **Mohamed Jassim Al Rais, well-known businessman of the United Arab Emirates. Branch: Travel Industry.**

In our culture you do not put the bottom of your shoes in front of me, it's like walking on dirt! That's not good! It's a sign of disrespect. Especially when you sit with respectful people, you shouldn't do that. – **Badria Almulla, prominent businesswoman from a big business family of the United Arab Emirates, active in diverse fields of business.**

The Arab Business Code (ABC): Showing the soles of your feet is an insult to your Arab business partner! No matter how cosmopolitan this lady or gentleman may be, however modern or open. It is also not a question of age – I know many business people of the younger generation who would be greatly insulted if you exposed the bottoms of your shoes to them, because the soles of your shoes reveal the lowest point of your body. And what the bottom of shoes also shows is "dirt." This can, as we already mentioned, put an abrupt end to business negotiations, or even cause a bad atmosphere for talks in the conference room. Both things can damage the business relationship with the Arab partner.

Try this: For meetings with Arab business partners, develop the following ritual: when you arrive, after greeting your counterpart and sitting down, place both feet firmly on the ground. Crossing our legs when we sit down is automatic for many people. So, it's best to perfect this ritual before your first meeting with the Arab business partner.

Cultural no-go ABC 2: Handshakes

> *If a woman has some reservations, she will not shake hands. It stems from a culture where women shouldn't see anybody but their husbands or relatives. It's a family culture.* – **Dr. Abdulrahman Alzamil, prominent businessman of a large Saudi Arabian business family, active in diverse areas.**

CASE STUDY

This reminds me of a story told to me by a businesswoman from the Arab Gulf. This woman travels the globe evaluating investments and regularly negotiates with men from all parts of the world; here, we're talking about a very open minded modern Arab woman. But when it comes to handshakes, she goes back to her culture and tradition. She just doesn't want to shake hands! And how does she make this clear to international businessmen? While greeting them, she crosses her hands over her chest; some business people don't understand this gesture – then she still has to shake hands.

The Arab Business Code (ABC): Never assume that Arab businesswomen will shake your hand! Touching hands is considered a very intimate gesture in this culture. You need to understand this. The same goes for men: many Arab business men will not shake the hand of someone of the opposite sex.

Try this: During the greeting, wait and see how your Arab business partner acts toward you. What are his or her signals – are they extending their hand, or not? You should be able to wait patiently for this, and then respond to their reaction. This approach creates a relaxed situation, with no stress.

Don't get me wrong, that fact that you've stretched out your hand to greet your Arab counterpart, and invited him to shake it, is not going to make or break the deal. But being considerate of the "cultural no-go" is going to put you in a stronger position and set you apart from the competition. Because, through your actions, you're displaying respect toward your Arab counterpart.

One more tip: If you hold out your hand to the Arab business partner, remember not to squeeze too hard, because a firm handshake that is viewed in the western world as a sign of honesty and straightforward-ness could be too strong for Arab counterparts. They tend to have very gentle, soft handshakes.

Cultural no-go ABC 3: Eye contact

Some of our people do not look straight into a woman's eyes – it hap-pens. And lowering their eyes is being respectful of the lady and doesn't mean they're looking at something else. So, the lady will not feel strange and think she's being ignored. You need to know it's a sign of respect. They respect you. – **Badria Almulla, prominent businesswoman from a big business family of the United Arab Emirates, active in diverse fields of business.**

CASE STUDY

It happened to me, I remember when I started out in the United Arab Emirates, I'd been invited to the Dubai World Cup, one of the most prestigious horse races in the world. I was invited into the lounge of a highly reputable Arab businessman – for a meeting. And when I stood across from him, he suddenly cast his eyes to the ground. I was surprised and shocked at the same time; it made me totally insecure. And I asked myself: "What have I done wrong? Does this man have a personal prob-lem with me?" I had an extremely unpleasant feeling.

The Arab Business Code (ABC): As the Arab businesswoman said in the beginning: Some Arab businessmen, if they are especially con-servative, will avoid eye contact with female business partners – also in meetings they will focus their eyes on the male colleagues, so as not to send the wrong message. Whereas in the western world direct eye contact between men and women is standard practice, and not viewed as offensive or reputation damaging, in the Arab Gulf this type of behavior could signal, to men who are very conservative, an indirect invitation to engage with this woman in an "intimate" relationship. And this, in turn, could lead some people to think the woman in question is an "easy catch." Otherwise this man wouldn't risk behaving in such a way, as it would mean dishonoring the woman.

Keep in mind: Every kind of encounter between Arab men and women in the Gulf, is always very carefully considered – sensitive and thoughtful. Especially in public, a certain distance is preserved, even when it comes to eye contact. No one wants to be in the least compromised. This type of behavior is also part of the cultural code of people in the Gulf.

Try this: Should you, as an international businesswoman, find yourself in a situation like this – where your Arab counterpart is not looking at you, or concentrating only on the male colleagues throughout the whole meeting, then there's only one thing to do: just accept it! And don't take it personally. Even if the Arab businessman is not looking straight at you, he's paying attention to you, indirectly – the whole time. He's just communicating on a different level with you. For, as the Austro-American philosopher and psychologist Paul Watzlawick wisely notes: "One cannot *not* communicate," because any kind of communication (not only with words) is a form of communication in and of itself, even being silent. So, it's impossible not to communicate. Remember this!

CHAPTER 5

Communication culture
with the Arab Business Code

We are driven in our communication mainly by our emotions, respect, and our first look at people. – **Businesswoman from the United Arab Emirates, active in many areas of business.**

It goes like zig-zag – I take a position; you go a little to the right. Then you take a position and I move a little bit to the left. Then you turn right. And finally, we find each other. – **Dr. Abdulrahman Alzamil, prominent Saudi Arabian businessman, member of a big family business, active in diverse fields of business.**

Keep in mind: You need to master a completely new form of communication with people from the Gulf.

What you need to know: Communication culture plays a key role in the Gulf, as the locals are a very verbally oriented society. Here people like to discuss, brainstorm and chit-chat all the time, even in business. As a result, it needs to be mastered, by any means, especially as locals of the Gulf communicate in a way we are not at all accustomed to. Visitors need to be aware of this.

This is what international business people say:

One of the things that took me a long time to figure out was their thinking process. Sometimes people from outside assume that everybody is taught to think in a direct way – 1,2,3. And there are causes and effects. But especially here, in the Arabian Gulf, one has nothing to do with the other. That's their logic. It's just another approach. – **American businessman. Branch: Transport and Logistics.**

CASE STUDY: *Abrupt change of topic*

This is what Arab business people say:

> *For example, once we had a briefing for Saudis. Suddenly one of the Saudis from the audience raised his hand and said, "We understand all of this. Fixing our whole time structure. And by the way, on page 53 of your briefing, there were graphics. Can we talk more about this chart?" We were surprised and asked ourselves, "Where did that come from? Why is he asking this now?" One thing had nothing to do with the other.* – **American businessman, active in different business fields.**

The Arab Business Code (ABC): It is this special communication code in the Arab Gulf of constantly switching subjects – even during business meetings – that makes communicating with locals challenging. International business people, on the other hand, try hard not to get lost and prefer to stick to the actual topic and the deal in question. But at the same time, it also makes it more interesting if one does not focus solely on the business matter, if there is room for spontaneity. You can also put them on the spot with personal questions. An example is: "How are you doing?" or, "How is your family?" A few seconds later, the Arab counterpart will address the business issue again. But still you're not settled; suddenly, he switches again, moving back to the private level, asking another personal question. A few sentences of this and it's a sharp turn back to business again.

Let me put it in a more "pictorial" way: communication in the Gulf is like riding a roller-coaster. The dynamics of changing subjects can be very emotionally exhausting, like being at the top of a roller coaster and then nosediving, full speed ahead, without stopping for a second. These emotions can cause confusion, and create exactly the kind of sensations that, especially with emotionally driven people, can cause business meetings to go astray, because the people on the "roller-coaster" forget the real reason they came – to discuss business. This can happen, for example, when they are invited to meet high-ranking royals or sheikh's families for the first time, as these encounters can be quite impressive.

CASE STUDY: *Using the Majlis for business opportunities*

I recall one moment of decoding while visiting an international business giant in the Gulf: The international businessman was invited to a magnificent *Majlis* ("place of sitting") of a United Arab Emirates sheikh – imagine an enormous space with golden chandeliers, totally spectacular. Judging by the amazed expression on his face, this businessman was obviously impressed. After the traditional greeting ceremony, the sheikh asked him to come and sit on his right side (this is the place for the guest of honor, a gesture of great respect). From this spot, the businessman had the best starting position for a private discussion with the sheikh; now, he could tell the sheikh more about his proposal and the financing required. But it appeared as if the international businessman was letting this huge chance slip; it seemed he wasn't familiar with the local technique of communication, because during the conversation he never managed to go from the private to the business aspect, even though the sheikh was leaving him plenty of room to do so, placing the ball in his court with phrases like: "Health is very important to my wife and me," or, "We plan to visit a health spa in Europe, to get a full health check." These are special moments the businessman should have been aware of – he should have taken the leap to change to the "level of business." But he did not know how to bridge this topic – a research project on health for which he was looking for investments – with what the sheikh was referring to, the visit to a spa with his wife. The businessman missed the opportunity to deliver solutions suited to the needs of the sheikh. Ten minutes of small talk with the businessman passed, then the sheikh got up, thanked him for his visit and politely excused himself. Suddenly, the businessman realized he had missed his chance. Now he had to set up a new meeting with the sheikh because he completely forgot to arrange for one during their talk.

Something to consider: Without a doubt, it's easy to be seduced and lose your footing in the magnificence of a sheikh's *Majlis* especially if it's the first time you've come face-to-face with a sheikh. These gentlemen know how to present themselves most honorably, with their impressive clothing and majestic appearance. Even the most experienced business people can be thrown off course in their presence; that's understandable.

But professionals in Arab Business Code communication techniques have the skills to stick with their plan. They always manage to direct the conversation back to the topic of business. Successful entrepreneurs in the Gulf never forget why they came in the first place. They let themselves be drawn fully into the conversation to ensure a dynamic conversation with their counterparts, which in turn provides a stable basis for moving business issues forward and ensuring good chemistry between themselves and their local business associate. This sets them apart from their competitors. One day, hopefully, you too will be just as successful!

Mastering communication culture with the Arab Business Code has many benefits: it allows you to deliver your opinions and present the matter at hand in an indirect, yet charming and clever way. Sometimes you "pack" this information into tiny anecdotes, from the perspective of a "third party." Let's look at an example of this.

CASE STUDY: *The finance department is having problems*

This is what international business people say:

> We had been waiting a long time for payment from an Arab enterprise we had worked with for years. I knew the owner and realized I couldn't place an angry call to him, even though I was mad that the transfer still hadn't been made. I had to be patient and arrange to meet the owner "by chance," by showing up somewhere I knew he would be.
>
> One day it happened. I stood facing the Arab businessman, engaged in calm small talk, and asked him politely, "How are you? We haven't seen each other in such a long time." He was very happy to see me and told me all about his family. Then he asked me, "How's business?" "Good," I replied, "but we're having some trouble with delayed payments."
>
> During our conversation, I gave him the impression of hopelessness. The change in the tone of my voice made it clear that I had a serious problem with this. I highlighted my frustration by saying, "The finance department is having problems with the transfers." This sentence I let sit between us for a little while, waiting to see his reaction; had my message reached him?

The Arab businessman knew exactly what I was referring to, and immediately turned red. He quickly changed the subject and chatted about his family again; then we politely said goodbye. The next day I got a call from my finance department: "The check has arrived." The Arab businessman had transferred the money after we met, that same day. – **Jean-Pierre Simon, Swiss manager. Branch: Hotel Industry.**

What you need to know: This example nicely demonstrates how to be smart about applying the communication culture with the Arab Business Code – finding a tactical way to reach your goal. You provide the important clues about your concern, but indirectly. And then you leave the person you are addressing free to decide if they want to deal with it or not. If they are not "ready" for it, and ignore your hint, then you pull back and switch to another subject.

Main rule of Arab Communication Culture

Talk directly about the things that need to be clarified. Be direct, but in a sensitive way, since you do not want to lose face, or appear in an embarrassing light. And, of course, you want to make sure the person you are speaking to also doesn't lose face. So, you do not get too intimate, expose or insult him in even the slightest way. While doing this, you should remain genuine and true to yourself, and state your proposal clearly. That's the main rule of communication within the Arab Business Code.

Let's take a closer look at communication culture with the Arab Business Code – and the strategies behind it. From the cultural origins of this communication technique, one thing is clear: through it the local businessman has the opportunity to get to know the person he is talking to better, and he does this one step at a time, with the just mentioned special kind of "chatting" (see 5.2 "Small Talk with the Arab Business Code"). Through many interlinked questions the Arab businessman learns a lot about his counterpart, such as where he is from and who he already knows in the Gulf. From these first details he can begin to build a foundation. Then he will do some additional research and find out more about his future international partner.

People from the Gulf are especially diligent when it comes to background checks. They make use of diverse channels. One of them is this communication culture with the Arab Business Code.

This is what international business people say:

Here, you can't do business like in Europe: placing an agenda on the table and just starting in on the business, that will not work. When you begin here, the Arab business partners lead the talks with personal conversations, on a private level. It's like a test: who are you, do you fit into the family, what can you offer? Are you doing something for the country? Are you married? Here they are trying to figure out exactly who they are dealing with. And if you don't pass "the test," you can't move on. – **Feridun Karaali, German manager. Branch: Construction Machines.**

This is what Arab business people say:

When you're talking I'm listening to you. How you're talking, what you're saying, who you know – all this information creates a picture of you. – **Ahmad Almutlaq, well-known Saudi Arabian businessman who is active in diverse fields of business.**

What's important in the Arab business world is you need to build a personal relationship with the people you want to do business with. Before getting down to business you enquire about their family and about their interests – whether it is sports, motorcars or horses, etc. It is important to build a personal relationship, and get to know each other better, and develop mutual friendship and trust before you do business. – **Dr. Mohammed Al-Barwani, prominent businessman of a large Omani business family, active in diverse areas.**

It's always about creating a good atmosphere.

Success stories from the Arabian Gulf have shown that international business people, regardless of the circumstances or cultural origin of their business, or products and services they offer, have one thing in common: in their interactions with locals they all adhere to these very specific building blocks of communication.

So, let's take a closer look at these building blocks.

5.1 SILENCE WITH THE ARAB BUSINESS CODE

As strange as it may seem in such a talkative world as the Gulf, silence is another component of success in the communication culture with the Arab Business Code. Here's an example.

Benefits of using silence

CASE STUDY: Let's have a coffee break – silence. And how much will the project cost?

I was sitting with an Arab businesswoman from the Gulf States. We were in her *Majlis*. I wanted to win this woman over to invest in my project. After talking about the family for a few minutes and telling her about my new project, suddenly, in the middle of our conversation, she waved for her coffee server to bring us Arabian coffee. It seemed the Arab woman had put a stop to our conversation; like stepping on the brakes. And I sensed she needed a break from all the facts and figures. On an intuitive level, it was clear to me: this woman needed time to process my input. So, I gave her that time, respected her unspoken wish. For a few minutes we did not say a single word, we just sat there in silence; you begin to feel very uncomfortable and strange, you're stuck in time. Even a second can seem very long in a situation like this. But you must remain firm in this and continue with the silence. And then, suddenly, out of nowhere, the Arab woman asked me the essential question: "How much will the project cost?"

What's important about silence with the Arab Business Code is, even though Arab business people from the Gulf are very good story tellers, sometimes they can't find the right words at a particular moment. Or maybe it is their respect for the people sitting opposite them, which I've already mentioned, that prevents them from speaking directly. Perhaps it stops them from saying what they really think about their counterparts. Suddenly, everything freezes up in them. In these circumstances they can't find the right words. As a result, a "vacuum" sets in, which needs to be filled with something. And a tried and tested filler has always been silence. So, let silence work for you.

This is what international business people say:

> *To say nothing, once, and see what happens, gives us entrepreneurs the opportunity to let Arab business people take the initiative. That's when it gets really interesting.* – **Martina Schwarz, Austrian businesswoman. Branch: IT Industry.**

What you need to know: Silence is incredibly effective since it gives both parties the option of reflecting on what has just happened, so they can "digest" everything they have said and heard. This period of "rest" gives both parties a chance to look at the situation more objectively, and to develop a certain calmness. It is an enormous help in the decision-making process, for both sides, especially when facing long-term, important choices.

Added benefits of using silence with the Arab Business Code (ABC)

Employing silence – and waiting to see what my Arab counterpart will say – gives me four marked advantages:

1. Better insight into my counterpart's frame of mind at the time. It helps me understand how much of what I have said has reached him. This can often be totally different from what I expected.
2. With the building block of silence, I am displaying self-confidence to my counterpart; I don't need to go into any further explanations because I am confident in myself and in my work, as well as in my product or service. This in turn creates a stable foundation for business cooperation, as my confident behavior ensures the person sitting across from me that she has made the right decision in choosing me as a business partner. This creates trust.
3. Being silent is also an expression of respect toward my counterpart, as I am prepared to hear someone else's opinion.
4. Through my silence I give the person I am facing the chance to impose their own view on the matter. That's a strong sign of trust, and one especially valued by people from the Arab Gulf.

5.2 SMALL TALK WITH THE ARAB BUSINESS CODE

Of course, small talk is not a cultural skill exclusive to the Arab world. This phenomenon of "casual chatting" takes place in every language and culture. But, still, small talk has its own code in the Arab business world, and this, you definitely need to know!

CASE STUDY: *Creating a relaxed business atmosphere*

Businessman Thomas W. from Europe was well prepared to negotiate a huge contract with a Saudi Arabian businessman. At first the Saudi seemed to be polite, but reserved at the same time, almost cautious. But when the European began to start chatting in depth about his own family, the whole atmosphere became more relaxed, slowly both businessmen gently reached the subject of working together. In between they still switched from business back to the topic of family, especially when they came to a particularly delicate point in their negotiations. In those moments the European changed the channel back to small talk to lower the pressure of difficult subjects and reduce the stress. At the end of their conversation, the Saudi tapped the European on the shoulder and said, "You will be very successful in our country!" Five minutes after the European left the office of the Saudi businessman, his phone rang and there was a text message from the Saudi with an invitation to his home for dinner. The next business meeting took place a few weeks later. The following month, the European was paid and the goods were delivered to his Saudi Arabian partner.

What you need to know: To get a better sense of "small talk within the Arab Business Code" you need to start with the history of the people in the Gulf region, in the place where everything began – the desert. Imagine nomads traveling for hours along hot, sandy dunes. Suddenly, someone appeared on the horizon! They stood face to face, meeting a stranger for the first time. There were no iPhones to allow for an instant background check on the person you just met. You relied on your own devices to find out, quickly, if this other person was a friend or an enemy.

The best method to discover this, was to invite the stranger back to your tent. Try to get to know him over some Arabian coffee and dates. Talk casually. A strategically clever mode of questioning came into being: small talk with the Arab Business Code. This technique didn't present the danger of appearing too pushy and intense, because, small talk is done in small steps. It is the careful "sounding out" of diverse topics, especially those of a personal nature. It enables you to learn details about your guest: where he is from, or if he belongs to a big family clan.

Well-mastered small talk with the Arab Business Code not only includes questions about their family relations (to which family your counterparts belong), it also creates opportunities to identify the person's connections and networks in their country. Consequently, you can learn a lot about the background of the people you meet. At the same time, you also find out what contacts they have, and this information is especially beneficial in business. All these gathered facts help you and your Arab counterpart form a better overall picture and profile of each other.

Benefits of small talk with the Arab Business Code (ABC)

Mastering small talk with the Arab Business Code provides you with many added benefits for reaching your objectives.

Benefit 1: Establishing a basis of trust with the local business community

The first sign of this is the Arab business person approaches you on his own and offers to work together.

CASE STUDY: *Just dropping by for a chat – without touching on business*

This is what Arab business people say:

Even if you don't know the key local decision maker yet, or you don't have a business relationship with him, you can still drop by his office for some small talk – just like that. And then you start chatting: "Good morning. How are you? How's it going?" And he will reply: "Hamdullah (thanks to God), everything's OK." The Arab business-man might not say anything at this point, but you keep on sitting in his office, drinking tea or coffee. At some point, you start chatting again and he will ask, "How is your family?" and you'll tell him. After a while you'll leave his office, say goodbye without having touched on any kind of business, without having achieved any results of a business nature.

You'll repeat these casual visits to the local businessman two or three times. During these encounters, you'll never say a word about business either. You are just dropping by to chat.

The first and second time, he will be somewhat reserved. By the third time, you can mention your work, what you do, what you have to offer, your successes in business. You do this the fourth, fifth and sixth times as well, by dropping by, just popping in for a chat.

By the seventh time, when you enter the office of the local busi-nessman, he will greet you politely and say, "Nice of you to come. There is something I need to ask you about your company . . . " Then you know: now you are ready to do business with him! – **Austrian manager. Branch: Special Vehicles.**

What you need to know: Building a business relationship with Arab counterparts is based on many unspectacular situations – without purely focusing on the subject of business. You get to know the other person, invest time in the relationship, and also leave the local business person the opportunity to approach you on their own, without any pressure. This is something people from the Gulf like to do, because they are curious, very, very curious! At some point, Arab business people will ask you about yourself. And with these first enquiries they will open a "business dance" with the international entrepreneur. And the ideal first step for such a dance is small talk as part of the Arab Business Code. It is an enormous help in setting this process in motion.

Above all, engaging in this small talk can help international entrepreneurs collect a lot of valuable information about the business needs of the potential local partner. These needs can then be dealt with accordingly and the Arab businessman presented with a custom-made offer. Therefore, invest lots of time and patience in letting the Arab businessman come to you on his own – without any pressure.

Benefit 2: Use small talk as an opportunity to address especially delicate subjects

The first sign: The Arab Business person begins to listen carefully, concentrating on understanding the business motives of his counterpart. He initiates the next meetings and is always present at these meetings.

CASE STUDY: *Vanished without a trace – how to sail around negative influences on the project*

This is what international business people say:

> *During a project, the technical manager of a Saudi company made life very difficult for the international partner. The technician was always trying to "orchestrate" a dispute with him and was permanently dissatisfied with the product. The international business person couldn't do anything to make it right; this technician was not interested in finding solutions. He kept complaining to the decision makers of the Saudi company about the bad work of the partner and little by little he painted a negative picture of him to the Saudis, presenting him as highly unprofessional.*
>
> *The international partner knew this but could not do anything about it. He couldn't contact the Saudi owner directly, because this would mean passing over the technician, and that would only have*

reinforced his reputation as "unprofessional." So, the international partner had to be patient and wait for the right moment – for a chance to meet the Saudi Arabian owner personally.

The day came, and they sat across from each other. Even though there was tension in the beginning of the meeting (the Saudi owner had naturally been influenced by the negative information given by his technician) with masterful small talk, the international partner created a favorable climate for discussion from the word go. He did this by talking about Saudi Arabia and its people and he invited the Saudi owner to visit him in Germany, to see the head office for himself. In between, during the small talk, he also mentioned a few helpful solutions to the production problems (solutions he had tried, time and time again, to explain to the technician). From this moment on, after extensive small talk, the ice between the Saudi Arabian and the international businessman was broken. The technician never got another chance to speak badly about the work of the international partner, although he kept trying; the owner was no longer listening to the technician.

Through small talk the Saudi had gotten to know his partner personally and realized this man was reliable and could get the job done if he wasn't being hindered by the technician. It was clear to the Saudi that the technician was never interested in fixing the problem, but just wanted to start a fight. After that meeting the situation changed drastically. The Saudi owner took over the conversations with the international partner. The technician seemed to have "vanished without a trace," he never showed up at any of their meetings again. The Saudi had "pulled him out of the game," so to speak.

– Austrian businessman. Branch: Electrification, Automation, and Digitalization.

Something to remember about small talk and using it with the Arab Business Code (ABC): By mastering the art of small talk you make it possible for the local businessman to get a better sense of you, the other side. Because for people from the Gulf, small talk is a kind of fact-finding mission. Therefore, small talk is a time-and-money-saving technique, which helps to secure cooperation with Arab business people.

Try this: Wait patiently for the right moment to apply your small talk techniques. Then you will find a mutual solution to any problems that may crop up – in a much quicker way.

Benefit 3: Use small talk to overcome boundaries – especially when it comes to tough price negotiations

The first sign: Your Arab counterpart tells you about very personal, emotional, circumstances that have significantly changed his life.

CASE STUDY: *Two old warriors – we need to find a business solution*

This is what international business people say:

I remember a really tough deal – the Saudi businessman wanted six helicopter engines for the price of four. He wanted a price and a schedule I could never deliver. It was like we say, "buying the business" – he'd win, and I'd lose financially. I couldn't afford to do that.

So, I went to the office of this Saudi businessman and sat down to have some tea and the small talk and chit-chat started. The Saudi had the model of a helicopter on his desk and behind the helicopter there was a picture of a very young man. I asked him, "Is this your son?" And he said, "Yes." I complimented him on how strong his son looked and on how strong his son's eyes looked and I continued, "What a handsome man!" I touched the helicopter and said, "Is he also going into the family business?" The Arab businessman replied, "In the family business, what do you mean?" And I said, "I know you're a pilot, and your son is in the military, so maybe he is also flying helicopters." The eyes of the Saudi sparkled – you could clearly see that he was very proud that his son flew helicopters. Then he mentioned that he could not fly helicopters anymore as he had a back injury. And then I said, "I know, I have a slight back problem as well – sometimes helicopters are not our friends!" I showed him my arms and told him about my crash. Then the Saudi stopped – and for the next minutes he was telling me how he had hurt his back. We talked about this for a while and then went back to discussing business.

After the small talk, we were in a much better situation to continue our negotiation – it felt like two old warriors had met. The small talk disarmed the Saudi. It was like, "OK, all of the defenses should now be put aside, along with all of the poker-faces. I have something, and you need something. We need to find a solution." Did I get everything out of the deal I wanted? No. Did the Saudi get everything he wanted? No. But we'd created an equal playing field. Honestly, it was a good deal for everybody. Not the greatest deal I had done, but an equal deal. – **Dale Karraker, American businessman. Branch: Aerospace, Energy.**

That is another nice example of masterful small talk in the context of the Arab Business Code. This American businessman was obviously brilliant at chatting, that much is clear, and I'm sure he did his homework before the negotiations started. He found out all he could about the Saudi businessman, otherwise he wouldn't have known he had been a pilot. That's exactly the kind of information we need to open up a smart, strategic and well-prepared round of small talk with the Arab Business Code. Only with detailed background information will you be able to drop appropriate hints such as, "Is your son also going into the family business?" or, "I know you're a pilot . . . " With these insights, the American hit the nail on the head and it led to moving on from business to an emotional level, a level that especially touched the Arab businessman and made him proud. And then both sides found something in common – back pain and plane crashes – life-changing experiences. That was exactly what the American succeeded in doing – finding a personal connection – thus perfectly preparing the ground for further serious negotiations. As the saying goes, "sharing is caring" or "birds of a feather flock together." Through this interpersonal exchange, both sides felt understood. This built trust. As a consequence, both were ready to reach a common business goal and support each other. People are simply human – that will never change.

Benefit 4: Use small talk to get better insights into the character of the Arab business partner

The first sign: The Arab businessman provides insights about his hobbies and passions – what's really important to him.

CASE STUDY: A particular brand of tea – to further cooperation

This is what international business people say:

> You go to a meeting and ask yourself, "How will this whole thing work?" You put your antennae out. And with the help of small talk you can really get a sense of a person's character.
>
> I remember a meeting with a top CEO in Qatar. It was one of my first business meetings with this Arab businessman in his office. Tea was served. After I took a sip, I said, "It tastes great!" It really did, I meant what I said. With this comment, I nailed it, because the Qatari began to tell me that he had especially chosen to serve me this particular brand of tea; that it was a family recipe. Then we

began to chat, exchanged news and had a hearty laugh. I noticed how funny the Qatari was and that we shared the same sense of humor. Our values and views on life were compatible in many ways. This good rapport, mixed with a relaxed and pleasant atmosphere for conversation, greatly facilitated our further cooperation. – **Austrian businessman. Branch: Construction.**

What you need to know: This case also illustrates how small talk can bring people closer – you exchange ideas, feel comfortable in each other's company and finally you even laugh together. In this first "getting-to-know-each-other" phase the potential business partner will provide lots of valuable information about his life. You learn more about him and can refine the profile of your Arab counterpart. You recognize what is important to him, what can build trust or, in the worst case, destroy it. You get valuable insights into the person's character.

The entrepreneur in the previous case did a good job. He was patient, put in the time necessary, and did not talk about business at the outset, but loosened up the encounter with some small talk, saying, "The tea is great." (Here, the importance of praise comes into play.) With this compliment, the visitor placed the ball in the Arab's court, who was grateful to catch it, as exemplified by his reaction: "It's a family recipe." With this response, the ball was tossed back to the European and the conversation was in play. Small talk with the Arab Business Code had begun. The local businessman was now ready to tell more about himself, for example, how proud he is of his family's recipe for tea. This detail too, is of great value, especially if, one day, you need to know what kind of gift to get your Arab business partner, what he will enjoy. It is always the small gestures that improve chemistry, they also help build successful business cooperation.

The Arab Business Code (ABC): Every serious relationship in the Arabian Gulf calls for in-depth knowledge of the other person. That is why you really must make an effort to find out more about the character of your future Arab business partner. After all, you are striving for a business marriage and would like to form a permanent tie. For this you need to know more about each other.

But many entrepreneurs are lazy in this regard, focusing just on the "outer shell," what they superficially perceive about their counterpart. They fall in love with the desired image of their Arab partner, just like falling in love with an attractive woman or man, without considering their mindset in more depth. But these desired people might not be the right partner. Just like the most powerful sheikh, prince or king might not be the right business partner for you. They might have values that are exactly opposed to yours. This can have fatal consequences later on – especially in the Arab Gulf.

That is why it's so important to learn about the personality of the potential business partner, and small talk is an enormous help in identifying these character traits.

This is what Arab business people say:

> *I met the owner of a Texan company and we chatted about life and her career. She spoke about how she built her own company, all the phases she went through and all the ups and downs. The way she spoke about her long-term partnerships in business and all the stories she told me about herself showed me very clearly: this woman is committed. Between the small talk I could make out her character, a character I would like to work with.* – **Faisal Al Hammadi, well-known businessman from the United Arab Emirates. Branch: Food Industry.**

I would even raise small talk to the status of a kind of art, as it provides access, in a creative way. Small talk enables us to get a deeper perception of our counterparts and understand them better. This is also something my years-long studies in the Gulf have shown me.

Some successful entrepreneurs even take this a step further and regularly train themselves in small talk. They realize this unique communication technique is a way to get ahead of the competition. An interesting approach that inspired me, as a researcher of successful communication techniques in the Arabian Gulf, is to ask two specific questions:

1. How do you refine the art of chatting?
2. And above all, how do you learn small talk as an effective skill, if it doesn't come naturally? What is necessary for this?

How to master the art of small talk – the first steps

Step 1 – The decision: First ask yourself a key question: Am I am really ready to learn small talk?

If the answer is "no," stop reading now, and skip to the next chapter, because when it comes to small talk there needs to be a genuine willingness to really engage in chatting with locals from the Gulf region (see Chapter 3.1, FITO technique).

Step 2 – The preparation: Before you begin to engage in small talk you need to find suitable topics. Set yourself the objective to compile the perfect small talk topics in a list. There are different ways to gather material for small talk and various techniques to implement in different meeting situations. Let's take a closer look at some of these situations:

Tool 1: Train your senses

Situation: Imagine you are facing an Arab businessman in his office for the first time. Your task in this technique is to always keep an open mind to your surroundings and be aware of the locals and their behavior.

CASE STUDY: *Watch out, even for small things!*

This is what international business people say:

> *The time had come. I was sitting in the office of a local businessman and waiting for him. I had time to take a good look around the room. I surveyed his desk and noticed that it was meticulously tidy. All the papers were carefully stacked in one single pile and next to this pile was a silver coin. That, in particular, caught my eye. After he entered his office and we exchanged greetings, he sent the cof-fee-boy off to get our coffee, and I asked him, "What is that beautiful coin there? It looks amazing!" His face lit up and he began to talk enthusiastically about the coin.* – **German businessman, active in diverse fields of business.**

What you need to know: This kind of "optical scanning" over the office of a local businessman always pays off, and it's quite easy to do. It reveals details about the Arab businessman as a person. Of course, it also provides great material for conversation, and helps you launch into skilled small talk with the Arab Business Code. But it's always your decision, if you want to understand the local.

Tool 2: Research

Be aware: It is essential for a future business relationship that you get to know personal aspects and characteristics of your Arab business partner in advance,

Situation: Picture yourself in a meeting with a prospective Arab business partner – you have not done your research and you have not gathered personal background information beforehand, so your knowledge of him is somewhat minimal. How can you succeed in initiating effective small talk at the last minute?

Try this: Open small talk by using only safe topics. Talk about the country and its people or the weather. That's always a good start, especially if you don't know your conversation partner that well. The reaction of the local should tell you what topics interest him or her, which topics cause them to open up and pour out information. These inputs from the locals are your starting point – continue the small talk from there.

It may happen that the Arab businessman doesn't react to your small talk topics. If so, let it go, right away! Accept that the local is not interested in this subject. He will have his reasons, and you don't need to question them.

For this "radical letting go" my Gas-Shift-Brake technique is very useful. It makes things easier during small talk; step on the brakes for a moment, shift down a gear, and then quickly find your way back to the main topic. Remember, this is why you are meeting with the potential partners in the first place.

Another thing I need to mention here, because it is so important: never forget to maintain a good balance, even in small talk. Which brings us to Tool 3 of successful small talk.

Tool 3: Preserve balance continuously

Be aware: If you are making use of small talk during a business meeting, it is essential to recognize the "turning point" – to feel when your partner is no longer interested in small talk.

CASE STUDY: *Tiring horse talk – sorry, can we talk business now!*

This is what Arab business people say:

> *I remember a meeting where I brought together a European businessman with a very powerful Kuwaiti businessman. After the official greeting, the European began to talk about horses. The visitor seemed to think the Arab man was a particularly keen horse lover and it was apparent he had prepared himself very well on the subject of*

horses, he knew a lot of details – from breeding to different kinds of thoroughbreds – and he spoke extensively of this to the Kuwaiti businessman. The local listened carefully for more than ten minutes, you could tell by his upright sitting posture and his fixed eye-contact. After ten minutes the first signs of "tiredness" set in: His eyes were not as focused, and, at some point, he even leaned back in his chair. But the European did not notice any of this and kept up his untiring flow of enthusiastic talk of horses. Suddenly, the Kuwaiti sat up straight, looked the European directly in the eyes and said calmly and very casually, "I'm very sorry, but I don't even know the difference between a donkey and a horse, can we please talk business now!"
– **Kuwaiti Businessman, active in diverse fields of business.**

What you need to know: A reaction like this is rare. Normally, locals never give such direct feedback, they retreat diplomatically. We've already discussed how the locals communicate their opinions and concerns, preferably with the help of nonverbal communication. The businessman in our case study did not intend to act disrespectfully toward the European at any given moment – that is why he listened patiently for ten minutes; even though he wasn't the least bit interested. But finally, there came a point when even this Arab businessman had had enough.

Let us examine this in greater detail. The European's approach was very good. He opened the conversation with small talk, in order to "warm up" the atmosphere – that was an important first step because regardless of how business oriented the locals are, a good mood is an integral part of meetings. The source of the European's mistake lay elsewhere. Therefore, let's take a closer look at potential mistakes in making small talk based on the previous case study. You need to know the Arab Business Code. Only in this way can you avoid losing your footing.

Basic mistake 1: Incorrect interpretation of body language

The European businessman ignored the body language showing the Kuwaiti's lack of interest. When his gestures became less enthusiastic, he grew tired and leaned back in the chair, it should have been a "red flag." This nonverbal call for action on the part of the Arab toward the European was a way of saying, "Please! Stop talking about horses. I'm not at all interested in this." But the visitor did not notice this and relentlessly continued with his barrage of words. It almost seemed as if the European was flexing his muscles at the local. In any case, he wanted to

Bloated Ego,
take a break!

demonstrate his knowledge and how clever he was, which was almost a kind of coercion – forcing the Kuwaiti, who did not want to hear about horses, to listen. Here's where one of the seven Emotional Hinderers in business life in the Arab Gulf comes into play: "the Bloated Ego." Be careful that it doesn't become too inflated and blow up more and more – "Me! Me! Me! Better yet, send the "the Bloated Ego" on a break!

The Arab Business Code (ABC): At the slightest nonverbal sign of indifference by the Arab counterpart, you have to step on the brakes immediately, and stop the chit-chat on the spot. Think of my Gas-Shift-Brake technique. Let out the clutch, shift back a gear, and start again with the basic focus, which is: how to succeed in business with people from the Gulf.

Basic mistake 2: A lack of research

In this case the European had not taken the time, beforehand, to find out personal information about the Kuwaiti businessman, he hadn't done his homework. If he had completed his research, he would've known that this local man had absolutely no desire to talk about horses. And then he certainly never would have broached this subject.

What the European did though, was let himself be too influenced by two of the Emotional Hinderers – one we already mentioned before – Bloated Ego. And there is another one: "Relentless Judgment," who always says: "All Arab people have the same interests – all of them" (see Appendix on the "Seven Emotional Hinderers in Business Life in the Arab Gulf").

The moral of the story: know the Arab Business Code. Don't assume anything about your Arab business contacts until you've checked, and double checked, the facts. Sweeping generalizations like, "all Arab people are the same – and are above all, camel, falcon, and horse lovers," are perceived as insults by people from the Arab Gulf. Like all people, they don't want to be known through generalizations. And such over-simplifications demonstrate not only your lack of interest, but also a certain disrespect.

5.3 HUMOR WITH THE ARAB BUSINESS CODE

Using humor in the Gulf region puts you in a better position, because locals like to joke among themselves, to exchange funny stories. It's a pleasure for locals to exchange humorous experiences and stories.

Business people who master the art of amusing conversation increase their chances of successful deals. Here are a few case studies of this.

CASE STUDY: *Do you know John Wayne? The shootout at the OK Corral in Arizona? Okay, then let's do five per cent!*

This is what international business people say:

We were working on a project worth many millions of dollars. It was a tough meeting. Usually, I would have a certain percentage for my Arab partner in my mind and he would consider a different number. He would write down a figure on a piece of paper and slide it across the table to me. I would think about it, jot down a different number that made more sense to me and then hand it back to him. This would go on for a little while. I'd be giving in a bit, and so would he until we reached a number we could agree on.

But this time I did something different. I stopped and said, "Excuse me, can I check something please?" And my partner said, very gracefully, "Sure, go ahead." I made a dramatic gesture of counting in the air, just like I was calculating with my fingers, trying to add it all up. Then I said,

> *"You know, I went to public school in Arizona. I didn't learn very good math, but what you're telling me doesn't add up to the same thing I had. And in Arizona it needs to add up to be the same."*

So, the Arab businessman stopped in his tracks and asked very enthusiastically, "You went to school in Arizona?" I said, "Yes." So, he said, "John Wayne!" I responded with, "Yessiree!" And he blurted out, "OK Corral!" I came back with: "Howdy, partner!" He gestured like he was shooting in the air and burst out laughing. Then he said, "OK, let's do five per cent!" Just a little sudden joke, and all at once the atmosphere at the table changed and felt totally relaxed. – **Dale Karraker, American businessman. Branch: Aerospace, Energy.**

The Arab Business Code (ABC): This is something my experiences in the Gulf have taught me: people from that region have trouble dealing with hour long discussions, where there is constant pressure. They become restless and nervous and that definitely affects the conversation and negotiations in a negative sense.

This is what Arab business people say:

Talking business more than 45 minutes makes you tired. You need to take some breaks. For example, if you're stuck in the room with somebody, just have some fun. Humor breaks the ice and often makes it easier to close a deal. – **Emad Al Zamil, Saudi Arabian businessman. Branch: Brick Industry.**

This is why local business people from the Gulf States often, and gladly, use the building block "humor" amongst themselves as well. An example of this:

CASE STUDY: *Wealthy businessmen fighting to survive – how much for this carpet?*

I remember a situation where I visited a very wealthy Arab businessman in his office in Qatar. A carpet dealer had also stopped by to sell the man new carpets and if I hadn't known just how rich this man was, I would've thought, watching him negotiating carpet prices, that he and his family were in serious financial trouble. "You're asking that much for a carpet; do you want to ruin me and my family? How are we supposed to pay for this?" the businessman asked. And the carpet salesman replied in a heart wrenching tone, "How can you say that? Do you know how hard life is for me?" Adding, "My daughter is studying and that's very, very expensive! But I have to do everything I can for my family." The Qatari businessman again countered with arguments about the expenses he had to face.

So, they went back and forth for over an hour, with touching stories of two men obviously warding off disaster, struggling to survive. The only strange thing about watching this conversation was, every once in a while, the men laughed, and you could tell by their facial expressions that these two were really having fun.

The Arab Business Code (ABC): For Arab business people in the Gulf, negotiating means enjoying the game! They feel totally relaxed, especially if elements of humor are built into the conversation. Brain researcher Dr. Jill Bolte Taylor once explained to me that when you introduce humor into your arguments, you shift from the rationally driven left half of the brain to the creative right half. This generates a "flowing feeling," and you can actually "let go" and relax for a few minutes.

Try this: Treat your Arab counterpart to this moment of rest. Believe me, he will thank you for it – by wanting to meet with you again and again. Not just for small talk but also for business negotiations.

Humor with the Arab Business Code (ABC) and its stumbling blocks

Even though humor has many advantages in business interactions with people from the Gulf, there are also many dangers lurking in jokes. This is because locals from the Gulf often completely misinterpret international humor. And, even worse, your jokes might seem like an insult to them. Therefore, it is important to know which topics should not be addressed when using humor with the Arab Business Code. Let's have a look at three of the ABC no-goes:

Humor ABC No-Go 1: No jokes in any way connected to the families of the Arab business people!

Even if you have been friends, or doing business together, for a long time – avoid this no-go at all times!

CASE STUDY: *The daughter's marriage – do you really think I'm that bad a father?*

I remember a dinner with a group of European entrepreneurs, where there was also one Arab businessman present. I'd known him for many years and in the past, we'd often laughed together. We had the same sense of humor. Also, this particular businessman had a very open attitude toward western culture and its values and modes of behavior, because he'd traveled extensively abroad. So, I was certain there were no boundaries I might exceed with humor. I was convinced of this and felt totally safe in all types of conversation with him.

The evening played out with lots of humor. At one point we reached the subject of "men and women." We joked about the beliefs of the young generation of westerners, the demands made by western women in their choice of men. My Arab friend knew that I was single at the moment and in the spirit of fun he said, "It's finally time we found a good man for you. Marry you off! And it would be best for you to marry someone from our family clan." We laughed heartily, both of us knew that this was all in jest. I went along with the joke, winked at him in agreement and said, "That's a great idea! And while we're at it, then we can marry your daughter off to someone from my country. That would be good too!" Again, everyone at the table broke out in laughter. The evening continued in this entertaining manner – I thought.

A year went by and I saw my friend regularly in the meantime. Then one day, I was sitting alone with him in his office and we were discussing a project and suddenly, in the middle of everything, out of the blue, as an aside, he said to me harshly, "You simply don't understand me." I was shocked and asked, very concerned, "What are you saying?" He attempted to avoid the subject, in the tried and tested Arab Communication Culture manner. He was uncomfortable, regretted that he had blurted this out, and said, "It's not that important. I wanted to speak to you about another project . . . " He tried to change the subject, but I wouldn't let him; I insisted on an answer.

Finally, he gave in, and let his emotions have free rein. "Do you think I would really give my daughter to some strangers in the street. Do you really think I'm that bad a father? A father who doesn't take care of his daughter?"

I stared at him stunned, I was shocked. I had not been expecting this reaction. And then he told me that a year ago, at the dinner I mentioned, I had said to him, "Maybe your daughter can marry an Austrian." And for him this sounded like I had said, "Maybe you can marry your daughter off to the next best man who comes around the corner. Some stranger, someone you run into on the street."

The Arab Business Code (ABC): No jokes in any way related to the family. Never ever! That needs to be clear – when you're talking to Arab business partners the conversation is always taking place in a different cultural context! No matter how well you know this person, no matter how close your friendship is, no matter how open this person is toward you, do not let yourself be fooled. People from the Gulf will never put aside their "codes" and values. This will always prevail and outweigh everything.

In the society of the Gulf States the family has an extremely high value. Locals see themselves as deeply responsible for their clan – this is passed on from generation to generation. The father, especially, as the head of the family, has the irrevocable obligation to ensure a strong future for his daughter, and that includes finding an appropriate husband – someone who will guarantee his child's security, a carefree life once the father is no longer there to protect her.

Humor ABC No-Go 2: No jokes touching on the national pride of locals. Even if they are only about regional dishes!

CASE STUDY: *Not so fresh hummus – I hope you realize I'm kidding!*

This is what international business people say:

> I was in a meeting in Riyadh with the head of catering for a Saudi Arabian airline. In my meeting with the Saudi, he asked me how my flight had been. So, I jokingly said, with a twinkle in my eye, "Great. But the hummus was not fresh!" It was so clear to me that he'd understand I meant it as a joke – as he was the head of the airline's catering and it's very well-known for always serving the freshest and best hummus. And I thought by saying the hummus was not fresh, it would be the same as sitting in a perfect living room and saying to the owner of this place, "Your seats are so dirty!" But looking at the Saudi's face made me realize that this man was insulted and took my hummus joke very seriously. So immediately, I added, "I hope you realize I was only kidding." And the Saudi replied, "Yes. For sure. I know." But the next fifteen minutes created a different atmosphere between us; our meeting was not really positive or relaxed anymore. It seemed the Saudi catering manager needed time to recover from this shock. – **American businessman. Branch: Manufacturing Industry.**

The Arab Business Code (ABC): People from the Gulf region are incredibly sensitive about subjects related to national pride – this sets off an alarm, a state of emergency. They are programmed to think this way. So, the shock of the catering manager was a natural reaction. It was very hard for him to view the comment of the American as a joke. I would go so far as to say that this feeling of shock even stayed with him on his way home, because, after all, he was the catering chief of a famous local airline. He did not want to "lose face," which is very connected to hospitality and this, as we have often said, is very important in this part of the world.

You need to be careful when you talk about anything related to national pride. Keep in mind that locals may not find the same things funny as you do. And this includes local dishes – Arab people are particularly proud of those.

Humor ABC No-Go 3: No jokes related to sex!

CASE STUDY: *Bikinis in Saudi Arabia – the reason to go to the beach!*

This is what international business people say:

I had a meeting in Manama, Bahrain, for a project. It was a large petrochemical deal between the Saudis and the British and Americans for equipment necessary for oil transmission lines. I was representing the Saudi customer, who had been a part of the government. And there was also a Bahraini consultant company, and their consultant was a Canadian, based in Bahrain.

The meeting was going along pretty nicely, we covered lots of material and technical stuff. The atmosphere was quite relaxed in the meeting, people where hanging their work jackets on the chairs. And then the Bahraini company sent their secretary out to bring some food, we were taking a break. While we were eating, we started talking about the difference between Riyadh, Manama, and Dubai on a summer day and one of the British said, "It's hot in all of these places, one is more relaxed, one is cooler."

The Canadian added, "Well, there is only one reason to go to the beach." The whole group reacted like, "What do you mean? To go swimming or boating?" The Canadian answered, "You know, I worked in a lot of Gulf cities, but what you don't see in Riyadh are bikinis." The room just went silent. The Saudi guys looked at the Canadian like he came from the moon. So, I tried to switch the subject by saying, "Well, bikinis are maybe not appropriate." But the Canadian continued jokingly, "What do you mean with not appropriate?" I repeated by clearly stating, "Just not appropriate." At this moment the Canadian realized what he had done and stopped talking about bikinis in Saudi Arabia. But from then on, the temperature of the rest of the meeting had dropped – the atmosphere felt very cold.

After the meeting, one of the Saudis, the general secretary of the decision makers, came to me and asked, "Dale, who is this guy? How can he make a joke like that?" I tried to balance the critical atmosphere by saying, "He tried to make a joke, but it wasn't appropriate." And the Saudi said, "Yes, you're right – not appropriate. But you need to understand, Dale, this deal is in trouble now, because of this guy. They don't want to do the deal because of him." So, I asked,

"What should I do? Should I call the head-office of this Bahraini firm to send somebody else?" And he said, "You may have to. The guy is really offended." – **Dale Karraker, American business-man. Branch: Aerospace, Energy.**

The Arab Business Code (ABC): Society in the Arab Gulf is highly sensitive to the topic of sex. And if you have the misfortune to address a conservative Arab business partner with such a comment, then you really are in big trouble. So, if you don't know your Arab business counterpart well enough, never make jokes of a sexual nature. In order to engage in this kind of humor, you need to have an extremely good relationship, to genuinely know the man from the Gulf. You need to be extremely careful.

Humor ABC No-Go 4: No vulgar language or dirty jokes!

CASE STUDY: *The Boston Red Sox*

This is what international business people say:

> *We were dealing with a sale from one country to another country. It was a very complex deal and we had an American guy in the room from the state of Massachusetts. These people have a very specific accent and are very serious about their baseball team. This guy espe-cially was as serious as could be, he was even wearing a Boston Red Sox baseball cap and a Boston Red Sox tie and he had Boston Red Sox stickers everywhere, even on his computers.*
>
> *So, we started the meeting. The Massachusetts guy made a pres-entation and every time he changed his screen, the Red Sox logo appeared. Everybody could see it. So finally, one of the Arab busi-nesspeople asked, "What is this Boston Red Sox? What is it? I don't know what it is." And the guy looked at him and said – using slang – "Are you fricking kidding' me? You don't know what the fricking Boston Red Sox are?" The Gulf man answered, "No, I don´t know. Is that a football team in the US?" And the Massachusetts guy got even more emotional and continued, "Are you fricking kidding me – it's a fricking baseball team! It's the best fricking baseball team that ever played!" I tried to calm him down, to make him understand*

the Gulf guy just doesn't know what the Boston Red Sox are. Then the Massachusetts guy realized that maybe he got ahead of himself with it – he smiled a big jokey smile and said, "Well, I don't know if he doesn't like fricking (at this point he stressed the 'k' in 'fricking' so it sounded vulgar), or he doesn't like the fricking Red Sox!" You could see that he was trying to make a joke of it, but all he succeeded in doing was making it worse. Everybody at the table looked embarrassed. – **American businessman, active in diverse areas.**

What you need to know: Sometimes people from the Gulf can ignore this kind of language, but only if the deal is really important to them. In this case, the Saudi delegation was so offended they got up and walked out of the room. Up to now, the deal still hasn't gone through, even though a lot of effort was put into smoothing out the situation and trying to continue with the talks and even though they promised they'd never bring this guy with them again. They tried to explain he didn't realize he'd made a bad joke, but the answer was always the same: "As long he works for your organization, we will not close any deals. He is very unprofessional."

Try this: Before you start telling a joke, step on "the brake" for a second. In your mind, go through the list of no-goes. If there's even the slightest hint of a no-go in regard to humor with the Arab Business Code, then just delete this joke from your repertoire! This might seem extremely difficult and complicated, but you just need to practice; be prepared and train yourself. And that brings us to the next point: training humor with the Arab Business Code

How to master humor with the Arab Business Code

Even if you are not a "talented talker" there are still ways to improve your humor. You just have to make specific preparations and follow the individual steps, especially when you are meeting your Arab business partner for the first time. For this you need to be exceptionally well-prepared. So, let's go through these steps, to master humor with the Arab Business Code:

Step 1 – The decision

Ask yourself a fundamental question: am I really prepared to learn humor with the Arab Business Code? And most of all: do I personally believe that I can learn this type of humor with the Arab Business Code? If your answers are:

- I don't think humor is a key factor in doing business.
- I feel very uncomfortable telling jokes and funny anecdotes.
- I have no interest in learning humor.

Or, if you have any other reasons for considering humor to be unnecessary, then I strongly advise you refrain from learning humor with the Arab Business Code. Remember my FITO technique (From Inside to Outside): if you are not one hundred per cent convinced, deep inside yourself, then it won't work. Self-doubt and disinterest hinder every kind of learning process.

Step 2 – The preparation

If, however, you are convinced that humor with the Arab Business Code can enhance your business cooperation with your Arab partners, then Step 2 is just the place to start. To put this into practice you need to know all no-goes of humor with the Arab Business Code. We've already mentioned four of them in this book.

Step 3 – Learn the techniques

There are all kinds of techniques to train your sense of humor. Let me present you with a particularly successful one here: "My cultural *faux pas* in the Arab Gulf."

The basis of this technique is to make fun of oneself and your cultural *faux pas* (mistakes): And you do this by speaking always in "the first person," about yourself. Therefore, you can never insult your conversation partner. This is always safe territory for humor with the Arab Business Code. Let's look at a case study on this.

CASE STUDY: *Yanni*

I remember my first steps in the Gulf region and a special meeting: I sat together with a group of Arab business people who were talking among themselves. They kept dropping the name "Yanni" over and over again. "Yanni said this" – and "Yanni said that." All I kept hearing was "Yanni." This made me curious. So, I quietly asked the Arab businessman to my right, "Who is this Yanni? He must be some big shot. Everyone knows him!" The local next to me burst out laughing and could hardly stop. And when he told his neighbor what I had asked, this man also found it hilarious. Soon everyone around me was laughing. What happened? I didn't have a clue. But, whatever the reason, the outcome was a great atmosphere; suddenly everyone was completely relaxed.

What you need to know: The word *"yanni"* translates as something like, "You get my point? You know what I'm talking about?" It is used by locals as a filler between phrases and at the beginning and end of sentences. It can help to fill gaps, vacuums of silence, when you, for example, just run out of words. Or when you'd like to really emphasize something. Then *"yanni"* is always a good alternative.

In any case, my *faux pas* was funny to the locals. That is why I still tell this story at meetings. It always gets a round of genuine laughs and cools off the business negotiations with Arab business people from the Gulf. Therefore, just be confident enough to see the humorous side of your *faux pas* – your slip ups. It will make your life easier, and also that of the locals you're dealing with.

This is what international business people say:

> *People from the Gulf appreciate it if you share something personal, especially if you admit that you've failed in a nice way. They appreciate that, because someone who's brave enough to joke about themselves is just saying, "I'm not so full of myself, I'm not such a hot shot." This kind of humor is always a good opportunity.* – **Dale Karraker, American businessman. Branch: Aerospace, Energy.**

But what if something does go wrong? What if you have a slip up? This can always happen, even after sensitivity training in how to use humor. You could get careless in a euphoric moment, and you could always overlook a stumbling block. And then "the milk is spilt," and you have deeply offended your Arab business partner with a joke, even if your intention was good.

It's an unpleasant situation, that's for sure. But here is something I've discovered: behind every "slip up" in behavior, there is a hidden opportunity to make it right again, just like every crisis necessarily leads to new ways of thinking. So, lets deal with this now.

How to turn failed attempts at humor into opportunities with the Arab Business Code (ABC)

Remember the case study where I deeply offended my Arab friend with my thoughtless comment: "Your daughter could marry someone from my country." My verbal "slip up" caused my friend finally to confront me directly. And, after a few seconds, when I recovered from the shock, I realized: many people find it difficult to show their feelings, anywhere in the world, and proud Arab locals, with their cultural background, probably find it twice as hard.

The conclusion: By airing his feelings, my Arab friend showed that he trusted me, he was able to be vulnerable with me. And that was something special

Then, another opportunity emerged. Through this situation my friend and I were able to take our personal acquaintanceship to a higher level. We benefited from this situation and talked about cultural misunderstandings in a calm and respectful way. Thus, we got better insights into each other's cultures. The local learned more about my, western, way of thinking and I got valuable information on the emotional world of people from the Arab Gulf. This greatly enhanced our empathy for each other's cultural background.

Try this: Use "mistakes in humor" for positive relationship management with locals.

Be aware: After any kind of slip-up in humor, your inner attitude is essential; if you genuinely want to make amends. If you are really interested in repairing the damage, then it will work. Because of this I am convinced only our inner honesty, our authenticity, will guide us in taking the appropriate next steps in rebuilding our relationship with the local. Remember always to keep a balance. Your actions in repairing the relationship shouldn't be too extreme (see Gas-Shift-Brake technique).

5.4 ACTIVE LISTENING WITH THE ARAB BUSINESS CODE

This is what Arab business people say:

> You know, some people have a strange attitude. They tell you what you have to put in your own shop – how it should be. But we know our own markets very well. We know very well what works or doesn't work for us. So just listen – and see the result! – **Businessman from Qatar. Branch: Luxury Goods, Investments.**

Listening is an important factor for success in international business. And not listening in the Arab Gulf is a huge stumbling block. This is best illustrated by the following examples.

CASE STUDY: *The know-it-all – ignoring leads to the loss of millions*

This is what international business people say:

> *The project head of an international company always thought he knew better than his Arab clients. Even though his Arab partner kept trying to explain his point of view, and attempted to make suggestions, the project manager didn't engage. He even went so far as to completely ignore the suggestions of his Arab counterpart, because he was absolutely convinced his way of thinking was the right approach for the Arab company – after all, he had years of experience in this sector.*
>
> *One day a point was reached: after numerous failed efforts to present his suggestions, the Arab businessman was tired of being ignored by the international businessman. He pulled back, lost interest and let the project manager continue to work on his own, do it his way. Then the day came when the project was to be presented for approval to the Arab businessman. After the project manager had gone over everything in the greatest detail, the Arab businessman said to him calmly and totally relaxed, "I'm happy to close the deal, but first you do everything I've already suggested. That's what you need to do!" And that's how it was. The project manager had to start from scratch, and all because he simply did not listen to the Arab businessman.* – **Werner Piefer, German businessman. Branch: Safety Technology.**

What you need to know: Even though this case study sounds like a fable or fairy tale, it's one of these true stories from the Gulf, where not listening had immense financial consequences. So, don't underestimate your Arab counterpart – just listen to him!

This is what Arab business people say:

> *Don't come here and try to make your product fit into our market – that just turns Arabs off! Just listen – and then we'll tell you if your company may be able to help us or not. If your product meets our needs or not.* – **Businessman from the United Arab Emirates, active in diverse fields of business.**

And here's where the opportunities for international business people lie, when you can rely on a time-tested sales technique, and that is: "I'd really like to understand my client!" Companies that want to be successful in the Gulf have to understand their clients' needs. You have to be wholeheartedly interested in your Arab counterpart – it must be the true motivation for business cooperation. This is the only way it works. Be aware that Arab business people will sense if you're serious about them. And, the Arab businessman wants to be appreciated by his counterpart.

Why "active listening" in the Gulf is so important

Listening attentively and being very aware of your counterpart is essential to every kind of interpersonal encounter. That goes for all cultural affiliations – any psychologist will confirm this, and it's proven that children who were not "taken seriously" and shown attention by their parents, have trust issues later in life.

But why is "active listening," especially in the Gulf region, so important for success? The answer is, for the Arab business person, the group comes before the individual. If you sincerely listen to the individual local, then you are paying attention to him or her as an independent person. Thereby, you are not only valuing them as a person, but also as an individual in their community, the so-called "we." This is also highly appreciated by Arab business people!

What makes listening with the Arab Business Code (ABC) so challenging?

So far so good, it all sounds fairly simple. You listen to the Arab business person carefully and thereby focus more intensely on him or her as an individual. What makes the whole thing harder is that there are particular ways of listening in the Arab Gulf, which run very contrary to our western thought process. Ultimately, many westerners have been trained, from kindergarten on, to speak concisely and get straight to the point as quickly as possible. In many western societies it is customary to directly voice what we think or feel. In the Arab world the opposite is true. Speaking their opinions directly makes many Arabs very nervous, it causes them to break out in a sweat, because their sense of politeness prevents them from directly voicing their thoughts and concerns. It's how they've been raised.

The so-called new generation of Arab business people who studied in America or Europe and have thus gotten used to direct communication, has much less trouble with clear statements to their counterparts. And, throughout the Gulf, I've met Arab business people of the older generation who aren't afraid to give a straight "no" in business negotiations, even though this is unusual for people of this generation, who are always trying to be diplomatic and often communicating on a nonverbal level. But, even though this group of "direct" Arab business people in the Gulf exists, don't take this type of behavior for granted. Don't expect it. Think ahead and realize that listening in accordance with the Arab Business Code is always a good investment.

Together with my research team, I've devoted years to listening with the Arab Business Code in mind, because there are many kinds of listening in the Gulf, in the framework of business talks – verbal und nonverbal. The technique I'm presenting to you enables you to understand the "packaged messages" of Arab business people, so you can read between the lines. And once you've learned this, you can interpret the most diverse situations correctly.

Let us examine three classic situations of "reading between the lines" here, with the help of case studies. This will assist you in learning to form an opinion about your counterparts, to understand what the Arab partner really wants from you, and what his suggestions actually mean, especially when it comes to negotiations.

Three classics of "reading between the lines" with the Arab Business Code (ABC)

Situation 1: What is my business partner trying to tell me – without speaking directly?

The Arab Business Code (ABC): Listen to their feedback between the lines and always remember: these people want to be understood. Respect that!

CASE STUDY: *Finally being "heard"*

This is what international business people say:

> *There was an American company with two CEOs. The chemistry between one of them and the Arab businessman was not working at all, for different reasons. The Arab businessman didn't see the value*

in the American CEO, and the American CEO didn't believe in the Arab CEO. During that time there had been no development and no decision making in their business projects, but the head office of the American company didn't react and went on ignoring the situation. In this phase, the Arab CEO was sending constant messages between the lines about his American colleague. For example, he hinted that maybe his American colleague wasn't the right guy for the job.

The whole situation got worse. Finally, the American head office decided to pull out the American CEO. After this man left, the whole situation immediately changed, and it seemed that the Arab businessman felt he had been "heard." Then things really got started; suddenly the Arab and the American businessman truly worked together. They made decisions instead of just talking about them. It seemed like the Arab businessman had verbally said: "Great, let's take it to the next level!" – **American businessman, active in diverse fields of business.**

What you need to know: This case study demonstrates clearly: from the beginning, the Arab businessman expected the American company to read the message he had hidden between the lines. He was surprised it took them so long. But when the American company finally acted and pulled the American colleague from the negotiations, the Arab felt he had been understood. He appreciated that the American company had finally respected his "signals." He perceived the removal of the CEO as an act of trust by the American company toward him, the Arab businessman.

This case study turned out well in the end. But, unfortunately, many international business people still have a hard time finding the "hidden message" in statements by Arab business people, which is perfectly understandable. It's a totally new and unfamiliar form of communication for us.

This is what international business people say:

At the beginning, it was very difficult for me because it's something completely different than what we know of business talks in Europe. All at once, in the middle of going over numbers, the topic of "business" is totally set aside. Suddenly, we are having meaningful discussions about racing horses and camels; that's what you need to accept, to learn to keep on listening carefully. Even if you don't know exactly what's behind this. You still have to take this chatting about private things and hobbies very seriously. Because, then, out of nowhere, comes a sentence with an implied meaning, where the Arab business person is trying to tell you something regarding the business at hand. It is precisely these small fine hints between the lines that you need to pick up on, in that moment; to know exactly what your Arab counterpart wants to tell you. That's why you have to listen carefully. And learn to read between the lines! – **Thomas Dreiling, German manager. Branch: Industrial Plant Engineering.**

One of the tricks is, the first things you hear are not what they really mean. You have to look for what's underneath. Because that's what they really want to tell you. – **American businessman. Branch: Transport and Logistics.**

It doesn't matter if it's during the negotiations or when the Arab businessman is telling his personal anecdotes, you still have to listen really well and learn to read between the lines. Pay attention to this! That's the only way you'll learn more about your counterpart. And also discover things that he wants to hear, or that are important to him, if, maybe, he needs more explanations before he can close the deal. You should pick up on these clues between the lines. – **Martina Schwarz, Austrian businesswoman. Branch: IT Industry.**

Situation 2: What's the true meaning of suggestions by Arab business people?

The Arab Business Code (ABC): It can happen that your Arab counterpart keeps repeating certain suggestions, over and over again. See this as "a red flag!" Take what he says seriously into consideration.

CASE STUDY: *Contract details*

I remember a meeting of an international businessman with a potential Arab client. The Arab businessman was insisting on details that should be included in the contract, but the international businessman was arguing against these, saying they made no sense, and he had a long list of reasons for this.

Even though the Arab businessman did not directly say a single word about it, I could clearly read the message between the lines. For me, it was almost as if he was screaming out the following words: "Put this detail into the contract, otherwise you'll lose the deal! I know my people. And I know this organization very well. And If you don't listen to me, I can't help you in this." The Arab businessman never said a word of this, but by repeating his suggestion to the international businessman again and again, he was sending him an indirect message: "Trust me. I know what I'm talking about!"

During the coffee break, I took the international businessman aside and made him aware of the "warnings" the Arab was sending and explained that this man was trying to help him, indirectly, to close the deal. But the international businessman didn't listen and ignored the Arab businessman's signals. In the end, he lost the deal.

What you need to know: It's very helpful to act on the hints of Arab colleagues you work with in companies and corporations, especially when it comes to internal changes. If, for example, a general manager is already internally promoted, but it's not officially announced, then you're a step ahead of the game, if you know this in advance.

This too my studies have shown me: especially in these situations, Arab colleagues are often sending hidden messages, trying to warn their international counterparts. Since these hints are, of course, not spoken directly, the messages are packaged in strategically clever phrases and asides. And by stressing certain phrases or words, these coded messages are pointed to "loudly."

What makes decoding these signals so difficult is that these hidden warning messages are often dropped at places and times when you least expect it. The coffee break between meetings is one such unexpected moment. Where you treat yourself to a little peace, after a tough negotiation, together with the Arab businessman, allowing both of you a few minutes for small talk on a personal level, taking a break from the mental pressure, and chatting in a relaxed way about family, hobbies, or what you did over the weekend. And it is exactly these moments when the Arab businessman – out of the blue – will drop a hint or send a coded message. And for we international business people, this is probably the least appropriate time.

I've always wondered why locals act like this. By observing their behavior, I've come to the following conclusion: it's exactly this relaxed atmosphere (drinking coffee, chatting, in former times they had even sat in the desert in tents) that allows people in the Gulf to come out of their shell and slip into their comfort zone. And this enables them to trust their counterparts. That's why they can send a "clear message," but in their own way, in the Arab Communication Culture. A clear message packed between the lines.

Situation 3: When doesn't the Arab businessman want to work with you?

The Arab Business Code (ABC): How can you tell that the Arab businessman is not interested in cooperating with you? A clear sign of this is when the Arab counterpart keeps suggesting other business partners for your joint venture. Here you must recognize and accept that the Arab businessman is staging his "exit scenario" and is no longer interested in business cooperation with you.

CASE STUDY: "I'll get back to you!" Don't they hear the bell ring?

I visited a successful businessman from Qatar and while I was sitting across from him in his office, he got a phone call. The person at the other end of the line was obviously trying to persuade him to finance a project, because I kept hearing the Qatari say, "Yes for sure – that's a great idea! Maybe Ahmed would be interested in it, or Mohammed, or ... " He kept on listing names of other people the caller should contact. These people, according to the Qatari, might be interested in financing the caller's project. That he himself might finance it, never came up. And he never once asked about the cost of the project.

What he did keep repeating was, "I'll get back to you!" I smiled to myself, because the constant repetition of the Qatari's phrases made it very clear to me. It was as if the Qatari was directly telling the caller:

> *"Please understand that I'm not interested in your project. I don't want to invest in it. Please accept that and let go of this. And let us end this conversation now. I mean now! Please! This is getting very unpleasant for me!"*

But the caller did not let up and did not respond to the Qatari's nonverbal cries for help. And the Arab businessman's politeness did not permit him to simply hang up. Somehow, he managed to end the call. When he put the receiver down, it was obvious he had sweat on his brow – he seemed exhausted but also relieved and happy the phone call had finally ended. He turned his face to me, asking, completely astonished, "Don't they hear the bell ring?" For him, he couldn't have made it clearer that he was not interested in business cooperation. So, why didn't the caller stop asking?

What you need to know: This is a very specific case study that I myself like to visualize often. Especially in those situations when I have my mind firmly set on something, when I am goal-driven and just can't let go. For example, when I absolutely want to win a particular business-man over to finance a project and I'm tempted not to hear the hints between the lines, because this businessman's participation means so much to me. Don't be misled. Even though the Arab businessman at the other end of the line is always friendly and cooperative, and even if he keeps assuring you how interesting your suggestion sounds and that he'll certainly get back to you, this in no way means that the Arab businessman is really interested in doing business or cooperating on a project with you. We've already touched on this – saying a direct "no" is especially difficult for Arab business people. That's why it's impor-tant, besides reading between the lines, to also understand the sign language of the locals, and to correctly interpret their body language. Let's look at this now.

5.5 SIGNS AND BODY LANGUAGE WITH THE ARAB BUSINESS CODE

In the past – in the desert – the language of signs was something people liked to use a lot, as I've been told by Arab business people. Back then, all these signs were clearly understood between fam-ily clans (the tribes). So, there was no confusion, everyone knew exactly what their counterpart was trying to communicate, what their intention was.

Reviewing desert "sign language" from the past

This is what Arab business people say:

> Certain signs were clearly understood. For example, when you entered the tent, the first thing your hosts would do was serve you a coffee. If you took the cup and drank it immediately, that meant: "There is no hidden

agenda behind my visit to you. I'm not asking for any help, money, or any other support!" But if you put the coffee cup in front of your host, that meant you were there for a certain reason, you needed something from this tribe. – **Doctor Aisha Darwish Alkhemeiri from the United Arab Emirates. Branch: Medical Care.**

So, back then, in the desert, things were clear without having to be directly stated. This even went so far that one could quickly establish if the visitor had hostile intentions or came in peace.

Understanding the Arab Business Code (ABC) with today's sign language

In the modern Gulf, many of the old signals (Bedouin signs) have disappeared in regional communication. The new generation, in particular, no longer knows the old signals. But, then again, there are still Arab business people who communicate with these signals from the past. One of these signs is the signal *"bakhoor."* Bakhoor is the traditional Arab perfume, in the form of small pieces of scented woodchips. When this incense is lit up, the smoking dish is passed from one guest to the other.

Bakhoor is often used at official receptions by the royal family and sheikhs – as a welcoming greeting but also as a sign of the host's respect for his/her guests.

What you need to know: If *bakhoor*, or *oud* as it is also called, is handed over for a second round (sometimes after the meal, dessert, tea, or coffee) it means the guests can leave now. The party is over.

In addition to signals like this, you also need to learn to read the body language of your Arab counterparts.

Learn to better read body language using the Arab Business Code (ABC)

Reading the hidden messages of local business people in their body language is also important for successful communication in the Arab Gulf. Likewise, not reading the body language can set off a chain of embarrassing situations in the communication with the locals.

I remember a situation that I can laugh about even today – because the whole thing was so bizarre to watch. But for the international businessman, this situation could have been very bad for business and a loss of precious time.

CASE STUDY: *The afternoon nap*

I'd arranged a meeting for a European businessman with a local. I'd heard that this particular Arab businessman didn't have a long attention span in meetings. He was well-known for enjoying a little nap around lunch time. Unfortunately, no other time slot was available, so we agreed on a twelve o'clock meeting. I briefed the European businessman, before the meeting, telling him to keep it short and concise. I told him about the Arab businessman's love of afternoon naps. And I also suggested we go over the presentation before the meeting, do some role playing and practice an "elevator pitch with the Arab Business Code" (a short presentation that should last no longer than the ride in the elevator, about thirty seconds). But the European declined my offer. He was convinced he could be successful – even without any preparation.

The day of our appointment came and, as the European sat across from the Arab businessman, reason gave to way to emotion. Everything we had discussed was suddenly ignored in the European's euphoria – he totally forgot our goal to keep it short, he talked on and on, losing himself in the details. During the European's extensive presentation, I kept an eye on the Arab businessman's body language. At the beginning he was very focused, leaning forward in his chair and looking straight into the face of the European. It was clear that the Arab businessman was fully attentive and listening carefully to the European, he wanted to know more about the business idea. But after fifteen minutes had passed and the European still hadn't gotten to the facts and figures of the deal, I noticed the Arab businessman making himself comfortable in his chair – the tension in his body relaxed, so did his concentration.

At some point, the Arab businessman leaned his head back, now and again, his eyes kept closing. It was obvious this man was getting ready for his noon nap! But the European didn't notice any of this, he was much too involved in talking. Now was the time for me to take action! A few more minutes and the businessman might have slipped off his chair. I "stepped in" and said calmly but firmly, "I think that's . . . " The suddenly unfamiliar tone of my voice startled the Arab businessman from his sleep, because he had been lulled by the European's monotone flow of words. He stared at us, somewhat confused, but then he quickly pulled himself together and sat up straight in his chair. Now his eyes were focused again, but this time they were directed at me. I acted as if I hadn't noticed the local dozing off and put the European's offer into a few words, keeping it short and to the point. Above all, I emphasized the win-win situation, the advantages this type of financing would have for him.

Then I asked the European to give the Arab businessman the handouts that we had brought along. And I said, in the same breath, "It'd be great if you could give us feedback on this at our next meeting." The Arab businessman looked at me, grateful to hear the words "next meeting." He was delighted because he knew it meant the meeting would be over in a few minutes. Soon he could devote himself to the nap he had looked forward to for so long. Thus, I won the local over as a friend, as I had orchestrated for him the classic "exit scenario with the Arab Business Code." Happily, he agreed. And as we were leaving his office, he told his secretary to arrange a follow up meeting with us. This next appointment did in fact take place. But before this meeting, I did extensive coaching on the presentation with the European.

The Arab Business Code (ABC): With their body language Arab business people are giving "signals" that you, as a business person, need to recognize already at an early stage. Especially when your counterpart begins to "drift off into his thoughts" during your meeting. And it doesn't matter if your partner is bored or just tired (it's understandable to be exhausted at these high temperatures – such as 45 degrees Celsius in the afternoon heat). The result is still the same: if you don't pick up on the signs soon enough, you can't take any countermeasures, or retreat with dignity. Then the meeting will have been in vain.

This is what international business people say:

> *I began to tell a large-scale manufacturer all my ideas and considerations. Soon I noticed that the local's eyes were wandering around the room, and he kept looking at his mobile phone. And I realized: this Arab businessman could only listen of for a maximum of five minutes; you need to see this in the body language. Then you will notice that this businessman is not following what you're saying and that he's telling you in a nonverbal way: "I want this meeting to end now!"* – **Austrian businessman. Branch: Construction.**

This is how the code of body language works in business in the Arab Gulf. Body posture, in connection with facial expressions and gestures, reveals the inner intentions of the Arab business person. In the worst case it means the person might want to "flee." So, to avoid these kinds of negative situations, you must carefully observe the body language. And if the local has a "desire to escape," then you need to enable him to do so. But in a diplomatic way. Here is how it goes: do not speak directly of this to your counterpart but accept his "flight" silently. In this way you save "two faces" – yours and that of the Arab business person. And you make sure that after "fleeing" it's possible for your counterpart to come back to you – with his head proudly in the air.

If this did happen and the Arab businessman in the above case study had actually fallen asleep, then his behavior would have been more than just a sign of weakness, he'd have been responsible for creating an embarrassing situation and would have "lost face." The result: the Arab businessman certainly wouldn't have made the next appointment as quickly; people tend to avoid those who have embarrassed them or made them feel guilty. Never forget that Arab business people have great problems with loss of face, because for them preserving honor and respect is always a priority!

But it's not only important to be able to read the body language and gestures. In the Arab world the "sign language of the eyes" also plays a major role.

The importance of eye contact

In the international business world, it is common to give signs with the eyes in negotiations. I would even go so far as to say that eye contact plays an even greater role in the Arab business world than in many other parts of the world.

This is what Arab business people say:

> *Eye contact says a lot about the person. The way the person looks at you shows what he or she feels about you. They literally express facts and figures with their eyes only.* – **Mishal A. Al Hokair, businessman from a well-known business family of Saudi Arabia, active in diverse fields.**

> *You always need to watch the faces of the Arab people – as we rely on eye communication a lot in the Arab region. Even in business the Arabs use eye contact continually.* – **Doctor Aisha Darwish Alkhemeiri, from the United Arab Emirates. Branch: Medical Care.**

Let us examine the meaning of eye contact in three concrete situations in meetings with Arab business people.

The meaning of eye contact with the Arab Business Code (ABC)

Situation 1: How to know when the time is right to change the subject

CASE STUDY

You're sitting at a meeting, talking about something and you're looking into the face of the Arab businessman. If you have the feeling you're looking at a mask – the eyes of the Arab businessman are staring at you – then it means the Arab businessman doesn't agree with you! Therefore, it makes no sense to continue discussing this topic.

My advice: Change the subject immediately and move on to another business topic.

Situation 2: Identify the group's decision maker

CASE STUDY

If you're in a meeting with a group of Arab business people and don't know the hierarchies at the table, you certainly want to be able to identify the top decision maker. Just watch the eye communication among the whole group; the group will guide you by always looking at the top person for confirmation.

My advice: After you've found out who the decision maker is, show and keep showing this person great respect. He is the "chief."

Situation 3: Identifying the decision maker in the father/son business constellation

CASE STUDY

It's sometimes even more difficult to identify the decision maker if you're sitting at the conference table with an Arab businessman, who's the owner of the business, and his son. Maybe you're discussing a new project with them and the father tells you in front of his son that he'll totally hand over this project to his son; let him be responsible for everything, that the son will be in charge of all decisions, even financial ones.

In this situation, it's important to evaluate the real power of the son, and if the father actually trusts his son to such a great degree. Therefore, watch the eye communication between father and son during the meeting carefully. How often does the father "nod with his eyes" in agreement, when the son says something? How often does he disagree? These reactions will tell you a lot about the true decision making and financial power of the son.

My advice: Even if you get the impression the son has decision making power and if you feel that he is your prime point of contact, maintain and nurture the relationship with the father. Because maybe, one day, it might be necessary to contact the father directly, and then you will need to have a solid relationship with him already in place.

Why Arab business people find it hard to say "NO"

We've already heard in this chapter (5.4 Active Listening with the Arab Business Code) how hard it is for Arab businessman to give a direct and clear "no." Locals hide their "no" between the lines or communicate it nonverbally with the help of "sign language" or a combination of body language, gestures and facial expressions.

But why do Arab business people act like this? And how can you more easily identify an unspoken "no." I've tried to find answers to this question, and here are my findings.

This is what Arab business people say:

> To voice a direct "no" hurts! Because why should I tell someone who's made the effort and taken the time to visit me – who's sitting across from me in my office and drinking Arabic coffee – why should I say no directly to his face? Or make a comment like: "Look, I don't like your product one bit!" I don't have the heart to say this! This person has done nothing bad to me. And above all, he's my guest. And saying no to him, it'd be very, very disrespectful. I just can't do it. I can't insult my guest!
> – **Hilal Al Busaidy, well-known Omani businessman, active in many business areas.**

I think the reason for this reaction lies in the way we grew up. First of all: we never want to hurt other peoples' feelings. And we don't want to create enemies, because we don't know when we'll need something or other from this person again. It goes back to our historical way of dealing with others. In the old times people lived in the desert, in tents. They lived on their own. And if they told other people "no, no, no" all the time, they would have left them. This would have resulted in people being alone and having to care for themselves on their own. But if they say, "I'll see what I can do, I'll try," they'll always leave a bridge, the possibility to get in touch again when they need these other people. So, the strategy was, and is: "Maybe I won't give him what he wants, but I won't say a direct no to his face." Even we, as Arabs, see that kind of behavior with our own people a lot. Rarely does anybody tell us directly whether they agree with us or not. They always answer our questions by saying: "OK, OK, we'll see!" – **Businessman of Kuwait. Branch: Law.**

What you need to know: The importance of always keeping a balance becomes apparent: one should never cross the boundaries of politeness. And never break ties to the others – "the group." This type of behavior was essential for survival, especially back when ancestors lived in the desert. And this survival strategy is deeply rooted in these people, even today. It is ingrained in many locals to never "shut the door." Always leave it slightly open, so you are able to come back. Also deeply entrenched is a sense of responsibility toward one's guest – this too prohibits saying no directly.

So, what should you do? And how would locals communicate a direct "no" to their counterparts?

This is what Arab business people say:

I will not say no directly, but I will lead you, in a nice and diplomatic way, to understand that I'm not interested. – **Businessman of a large Saudi Arabian business family, active in diverse areas.**

If I don't want to do business with you, I'd just stop communicating with you. I'd ignore your emails and wouldn't write back to you. – **Dr. Mohammed Al-Barwani, prominent Omani Businessman of a large business family, active in diverse areas.**

I think it's a talent to say no in a polite way – with a smile. And that's what I try to do. If I'm not interested, I usually say, "I'm sorry but I'm kind of not interested." – **Businessman of a large Bahraini business family, active in diverse areas.**

What you need to know: As you can see, locals react in their own individual ways: Some pull back diplomatically. Others say things like: "I'm kind of not interested." Words are chosen carefully. Arab business people are very aware of the power of words. That is why you'll never experience "a frontal attack" or expressions that could hurt or insult the person sitting across from them.

After years of studying Arab business people from the Gulf, I've developed three additional points that can help you identify an indirect "no."

1. **You need to be present:** Be a regular in the Gulf and personally sit across from your Arab business partners. Only then can you get to know them better and pick up on their nonverbal actions and reactions. This will help you to more easily identify their unspoken "no."

2. **Know the locals' way of communicating:** If an Arab business person is not interested in your idea, offer or suggestions, they themselves will not set any actions or reactions in motion toward you. It's a clear sign of a "no," for example, when they simply ignore your idea by completely changing the subject – unexpectedly. As you know, it is common practice in Arab culture, to avoid unpleasant situations by exiting diplomatically. And by exiting in this way locals believe they are expressing a very clear and understandable "no" to their counterparts. Unfortunately, international business people often do not get it. They are confused by this.

3. **Apply the Gas-Shift-Brake technique:** This technique, which I already strongly recommended for diverse challenges, is also very helpful in recognizing a "no." For example, when you approach your counterpart with your suggestion, then it's as if you were stepping into a car, putting your foot on the gas pedal; visually so to speak. Now try to analyze your counterpart's reaction and stay in tune with this for the next step – reflect. Then you either shift to a higher gear, or you shift down and tap the brake. This means: If the Arab businessman provides an answer to your request, then shift to a higher gear. If he ignores you, then shift down and reduce your speed, and let your request "cool off," by, for example, deliberately changing the subject. With the Gas-Shift-Brake technique you will always be able to keep things in balance. And to maneuver yourself into the best starting position. It will be then much easier for you to analyze your counterpart in their actions and reactions.

5.6 PRAISE WITH THE ARAB BUSINESS CODE

As the founder of psychoanalysis, Sigmund Freud, said: "You can defend yourself against attacks, but against praise you are powerless." Everyone likes to be appreciated for their positive qualities – especially Arab business people from the Gulf.

CASE STUDY: *Praise about important insights – "You know a lot of stuff!"*

This is what international business people say:

I had a situation with a Saudi businessman – in a meeting he acted offensively toward me. He was demonstrating to me how important he was. And that he had exclusive insights to things nobody else could have had. I was sure he was not doing it intentionally and that he had a reason for this kind of behavior. So, I said to myself: "Ok, that's fine." I didn't take his verbal attacks personally. Instead I praised him on his important insights, saying: "Wow! You know a lot of stuff! Very impressive!" This compliment about his knowledge disarmed the Saudi. And our meeting became friendlier and more relaxed! – **Dale Karraker, American businessman. Branch: Aerospace, Energy.**

CASE STUDY: *Praise of appearance – "You look so young for what you've accomplished!"*

This is what Arab business people say:

I was having a meeting with another Arab businessman, a pretty important guy. When I walked through his office door, I could already see from far away that he was quite young, in his fifties. He was wearing a toupee. And I understood in a second how important it was for this Arab businessman to look young. When I entered his office, the first thing I said to him was: "I just can't believe how young you look for all that you've done in your life – unbelievable!" The guy smiled, got friendly and the meeting was fantastic! – **Arab businessman from Saudi Arabia, active in diverse fields of business.**

What you need to know: Whether it's Arab business people or international ones, successful business people take the initiative and control their business meetings. They will not tolerate a "poisoned atmosphere," but take it a step further and become active. All of them are initiators of their business talks and will change any tense atmosphere into something positive. And complimenting the partner – praising them – is a tool that promises success.

The Arab Business Code (ABC): Arab business people demonstrate honor and respect toward each other. This is how social behavior in the Arab Gulf is structured. At any kind of gathering – something I clearly recognized in studying this society – the "show of respect" happens in the first minutes of the get-together. International business people need to be clearly aware of this in all their interactions with Arab business people. This is how their culture works: honor and respect are always a priority. And praise is one such mark of respect.

This is what international business people say:

> *You must always compliment something. For example, mentioning that the Arab businessman can afford an office in such a luxurious area, or stating the beauty of his office interior or how comfortable his chairs are, or praising the wonderful taste of the tea he serves. All that goes back to their appreciation culture. Respect your counterparts and show that you value them.* – **Dale Karraker, American businessman. Branch: Aerospace, Energy.**

> *You might tell your Arab counterpart: "We really appreciate the partnership we've had with you for so many years!" From the very beginning, a crucial part of any discussion with the Arab business partner is stating how much you appreciate doing business with them.* – **Kevin Cushing, American manager. Branch: Information and Communication Technology Services.**

> *It's so important to pay compliments in the Gulf region. You have to pull these things into the relationship with your business partner. For example, if I drive a Chevrolet and my kids drive a Chevrolet and I meet a Saudi businessman by chance who is the franchisee for Chevrolet in the Saudi market, I will say: "Hey – my dad drives Chevrolets, I drive Chevrolets – all of us are really big Chevrolet fans!" Then the Saudi will be very happy because I'm paying him a compliment. That's so important for doing successful business in the Arab Gulf. Otherwise it won't work.* – **Gregory L Black, American businessman. Branch: Hospitality.**

As you can read in the statements of these international business people, not one of them finds that complimenting their Arab business partners is a waste of time. And no one fears it will negatively affect future business cooperation. I've asked myself, why this is so? Because as I've noticed, in my coaching seminars, it is often men who see risk in voicing compliments. But why do these international people not shy away from this? What makes them so sure that their spoken compliments are taken the right way by Arab business people? I have asked myself these questions and have come to the following conclusions.

The three techniques of praise

Business people apply three techniques.

Technique 1: Successful expectation management

If you manage your expectations well, you automatically put yourself in the following situation: you don't take anything personally at your first meeting with the Arab business person! This might sound easy, but it isn't. Because, imagine what it might feel like to take a very long trip, and then finally face your Arab counterpart, and to sense, for example, that he seems arrogant toward you and has a "know-it-all" attitude. It certainly doesn't feel good! And it takes a lot of patience to not get angry and be able to praise your counterpart. This is the perfect time to apply the expectation management technique, because it will help you become more receptive to your Arab counterpart's behavior.

Try this: Put yourself in a calm, neutral starting position. The goal is to be aware that the behavior of the person you are talking to, at the time, has nothing to do with you; the local businessman is only struggling with himself. He's feeling "cornered," for whatever reason because, basically, it's very important for an Arab businessman from the Gulf to treat his counterparts politely and with the greatest respect. Therefore, enormous pressure must be the reason for this behavior, otherwise the local wouldn't react like this. But you can only have an understanding of this if you stay calm and balanced – and don't let yourself be manipulated by "Frustrated Expectation" (see chapter about the "Seven Emotional Hinderers").

Above all: If you master Technique 1, you no longer have to concentrate on managing your anger toward the Arab businessman, due to his behavior. At the same time, the desire to please the Arab businessman will be reduced – a need that is often essential to people seeking harmony.

Technique 2: Skillful profiling

If, as a first step, you can manage your expectations, you'll save time and energy and can focus one hundred per cent on this technique. Here you concentrate on just one task: to discover what's important to your Arab counterpart, what particularly draws his attention. Maybe, as in one of our case studies, he's an enthusiastic pilot. Or perhaps business relationships with family owned companies are especially important to them, and they are proud if these work out in the long run. It could be that something else has great meaning for them; you need to find that out. This insight can help you customize the compliment and come up with the perfect praise.

Arab business people from the Gulf are experts at this! They have a highly developed sense, which helps them come up with just the right compliment. They're not shy to voice a compliment, because they're aware of its power as a mark of respect and the "balm" of an effective and dynamic personal relationship.

Technique 3: Continuous balance in praise with the Arab Business Code (ABC)

In this praise culture it is also important to keep a balance at all times. Compliments should be used in specific situations and not exaggerated. Don't overdo it with the praise. Sometimes it happens, especially to newcomers in the Arab Gulf. In the euphoria of the moment, they can really "get rolling" and go too far.

CASE STUDY: *An exceptionally great airline! Seriously? We both know that's not true!*

This is what international business people say:

> I've made that mistake, I exaggerated too much. It was a while ago, in my early days. I met the owner of an airline; it was a startup airline. This airline was new, known for low standards. It wasn't in the best condition. Anyway, the company wanted to earn the respect of other airlines. And that's where I came in.
>
> We sat together in the office of the Saudi decision maker. The first thing I did was compliment the owner on the good job he was doing. And I complimented him on the exceptionally great condition of his airplanes, which in fact were not great. Today, I can't think why I overdid it at that time. The Saudi looked at me – and it was

very much the kind of look: "Seriously?" In fact, I could read it in his face: "I know you fly on international first-rate airlines all the time. I know you know what a good airline is. And now you're talking about how great my airline is? Why? We both know it's not true!" That was his reaction. He didn't say a word, but I could read it in his eyes and from his face. And then, in a split second, I changed the subject and moved on to our business conversation. – **American businessman. Branch: Manufacturing Industry.**

What you need to know: To sense when to "step on the brakes" in regard to praise is essential for business success. Don't get me wrong, of course, sometimes you run with the momentary euphoria, and one exaggerated compliment follows the next. It happens. And one compliment on the heels of another is still not a problem. But what you always have to keep in mind is that the second compliment should not be followed by a third, fourth, or fifth, to say nothing of the sixth. Keep it balanced! Because if you don't, then there's real danger ahead. Then you need to quickly think about using the Gas-Shift-Brake technique, where our "inner voice" clearly gives us directions, calls us to order and says in a strict tone: "Pull yourself together! Enough is enough! No more compliments! Get back to work!" And you stick to these strict instructions, and immediately stop "flooding" the Arab businessman with compliments, before the poor man drowns in praise.

This is what international business people say:

You're paying a compliment (you accelerate), then a second compliment (you accelerate further) and you're just about to make a third compliment (you're about to step on the clutch and shift up) – but then you stop (step on the brakes) and tell yourself: "It's enough! Don't overdo it!" Balance is so important in this part of the world, in the Arab Gulf. – **German businessman. Branch: Transportation and Logistics.**

Another thought: In the balancing of praise it is not only important to not exaggerate, but also to give honest compliments. Before you give a compliment, you need to be aware that, with every compliment, the Arab business person senses if it's really "coming from the heart." As already mentioned, the sixth sense of Arab business people is a significant communication tool for people in the Gulf. Only genuine compliments will have the desired effect on the recipient, the Arab business partner.

Beware of the Inner Critic –
the aggressive one!

What you need to know: The three techniques I just introduced – Expectation Management, Profiling, and Balance should always be considered when engaging in praise and applied accordingly. Maybe this seems like a lot of work to you, and hard to learn. That's why I've come up with a few easy steps to support these techniques, and help you perfect your praise.

Step 1: The decision

In reading this book, you've probably noticed the first step in all the techniques and exercises is always your own and genuine decision to really want to do something. This step, in my opinion, is the most crucial. It's where you ask yourself: "Am I ready to do this, do I want to allow a visualization of my Arab counterpart?" And here I must stress "want to allow!" It can only work if you have really made the decision and said to yourself: "Yes, I am ready to do this! I want to learn "Praise with the Arab Business Code!" Then you can move on to Step 2.

Step 2: A list of praise with the Arab Business Code (ABC)

With this tool you concentrate on the positive qualities of the Arab business partner. And the principal question in the preparations is, "What can I admire about my counterpart?" One answer might be, "I admire this person because he or she has managed, all alone, through their own efforts, to build up a business empire." Maybe this answer is not enough. Then you have to ask a further question: "Why does this Arab business person have such an empire in the Gulf? What distinguishes him, what makes him special?" Or, "How do other Arab business people perceive him?"

Possible answers to this question are:

- The Arab business partner has the ability to make quick decisions.
- The Arab business person acts as a role model for other powerful business people in the Gulf.
- This Arab business partner is particularly helpful.

As you can see, the answers can vary. Give your imagination free rein, and don't let yourself be influenced by anyone or anything. Don't let any feelings of insecurity seep into your personal list of praise. Above all, beware of the "Aggressive Inner Critic!"

In principal, an "inner critic" has a lot of positive aspects. Critical observation and analysis of the actions and behavior of the Arab business partners can be helpful in getting to know, understand and asses them better. In this way, an inner critic, speaking in a calm voice from within, can be very constructive to business, and also a sort of protective mechanism for international business people.

The type of inner critic you need watch out for is the one who speaks aggressively to international business people, who's always looking for the negative traits of the Arab business partner. This "critic" will whisper in your ear: "There's nothing good about this Arab business person. Absolutely nothing! This person is terrible! You can't possibly come up with a list of praise for them. That's not possible!" Don't let this troublemaker manipulate you. Don't even listen to this unpleasant creature! You can be certain no one has ever been successful in the Gulf by listening to the Aggressive Inner Critic.

Why a well-prepared list of praise with the Arab Business Code (ABC) promotes business

It's simple: from the moment you've made the decision to think about the good characteristics of your Arab counterparts, you begin to have a positive effect on them – without losing your identity in the process! This is a very important point for me: you attract your counterpart's positive attention but still retain your own point of view, preserve your own values. But – and this is the huge beneficial effect of this exercise – by visualizing the good characteristics of your counterpart you've mentally put yourself on another level. You've distanced yourself from the "stored up" anger and aggression against the Arab business person and thereby created a much more positive mood for the meeting. The dynamics are completely different now.

5.7 INQUIRY WITH THE ARAB BUSINESS CODE

Just like listening, so too is "inquiring" in conversations with your Arab business partners an integral building block of Arab Communication Culture.

As surprising as it may seem, Arab business people are often not even asked what they think of the presentations of international companies, or if they might have any questions. But why is this so? Why don't international companies try to respond to the needs of Arab business people?

This is what Arab business people say:

A lot of business people from the west are scared to ask direct questions, because they think: "You invited us here because we know!" Their mindset is: "We shouldn't ask any questions, as we are the ones who should know everything!" But that's wrong! That's the major failure for a lot of western companies – because if you do not ask, later on you'll make a lot of mistakes. – **Ibrahim Alkindi, well-known Businessman from the United Arab Emirates, active in many business areas.**

The Arab Business Code (ABC): Arab business people expect to be asked. It's true that you've been consulted by the Arab business partner because of your expertise. And it's also true that you must fully bring your know-how into the presentation. But once this has been done, the time has come to ask the Arab businessman for his opinion. This is an important point!

This is what Arab business people say:

It pays to ask direct questions, to listen, to discuss, rather than constantly trying to convince people about your ideas, your way of thinking. – **Businessman from Oman who is active in diverse fields of business.**

What you need to know: What this Arab businessman refers to as "direct questions" and what, at first glance, seems very easy to do, is in reality more difficult than you think. "Direct," in connection with "inquiring with the Arab Business Code," for international business people usually means something different.

Let the Arab managers explain it:

Here, in this culture, you cannot just ask the chairman of a company directly: "What do you want to know?" But you can inquire in a different way, for example like this: "Sir, what do you think – when would you like to do this? What is your opinion? Do you think that will work for you?" And then you say to the chairman: "I'm not sure if this is the right way, can you look at it and let me know?" – **Ibrahim Alkindi, well-known businessman from the United Arab Emirates, active in many business areas.**

Are you able to recognize this fine balancing act in Arab Communication Culture?

What's important is a certain undertone, how one invites the counterpart to present his view of things – respectfully, without any pressure. The moment your counterpart is ready, he will answer your question or make a suggestion. If not, he'll just skip your question and change the subject. It's something you just have to accept as the person who is doing the asking. Immediately let go of this line of questioning and turn to another aspect.

I personally find this form of communication great, because it offers both sides the freedom to decide on their own when they are ready to speak their mind. It reminds me also of a saying by Confucius: "Let go, what you love. If it comes back, it's yours – forever." You might ask what all this has to do with tough business in the Arab Gulf? Well, a successful business relationship always has two sides, and both sides always have to be willing to deal with questions. Only then can it work. And only then can something good come of it.

Let us look closely at when "inquiring" in the Gulf is essential to business success.

Pushing solutions through inquiries

CASE STUDY: *The fifth warning*

A European company had entered into a contract with a Saudi Arabian partner. In addition, another Saudi Arabian company was commissioned to service the delivered products. But this Saudi company did not cooperate professionally with the European company, and the problems that arose were always attributed to the Europeans, even though they were not at fault.

The European company described the problem to its Saudi Arabian client, and indicated that this could lead to major problems in the future, because, from the end consumer's perspective, it seemed the service offered was not good. But the Saudi partner ignored the Europeans' warnings, replying: "I know, I know . . ." For the Europeans it was clear, the warning had still not gotten through to them, and the locals still did not understand just how serious this situation actually was. So, one of the employees of the European company used the "inquiring technique." In the next meeting with the client, he kept repeating, again and again, the same message: A WARNING, which he worked into all his statements. Not once, or twice, but over and over again he kept coming back to that. The first time the Arab businessman replied with, "Yes, yes." The second time with, "I know! You told me that already!"

Near the end of the meeting, as the European was about to leave the room, he said it for a fifth time. With the following words: "I need to tell it to you again, because I feel I'm not getting through to you. But we need to do something NOW! Otherwise we will not be able to break this cycle and come out ahead. It is not going to get better!" And this time, after the fifth warning, the Saudi partner looked at him and said, "You know, I never saw it like that." In this moment, the European knew the message had hit home, for the first time; and not only in terms of content, but on an emotional level too. A few weeks later, the Saudi Arabian reacted and arranged a meeting for all those involved. The subject of the meeting was: "How do we improve the servicing of our product." The goal of the European had been reached. – **Austrian manager. Branch: Special Vehicles.**

What you need to know: As you can see, the European businessman used the technique of repetition. Pure information is sometimes not enough for the Arab business person. In this part of the world, emotions rule; only then will locals become active. In our case study, the Arab businessman understood the content of the European's warning, already the first time. The problem was he didn't "receive" the message emotionally. But by repeating and emphasizing the warning again and again, it finally landed on fertile ground.

Let's look at this in more detail: The first time the European businessman expressed the warning, the Arab counterpart responded with: "Yes, yes ... " The second and third time he said: "I know! You've already told me!" With this sentence the Arab businessman got a bit more personal. The fourth warning had almost emotionally reached the local. And by the fifth time the Arab businessman was ready – from that moment on he became totally engaged, and above all creative. It was the first time he realized the high level of the problem. And then he said: "You know, I never saw it like that." This was when it became apparent that the Arab businessman had understood and accepted the warning.

Successfully implementing this technique takes time. That is why you should not discuss too many points at sensitive meetings. Always remember, less is more!

The Arab Business Code (ABC): Don't have more than two topics on the agenda for your meetings. You might be disturbed, participants could be called away, new ones might join the meeting. So be careful not to lose sight of your goal and use the techniques of repeated inquires to reach it. To discuss further matters, simply make a new appointment.

Acquiring new contracts through inquiries

CASE STUDY: *The visualized cable car*

This is what international business people say:

> *I finally had a scheduled meeting and was sitting across from the potential Arab partner – we wanted to sell him our product and services. In this case it was a cable car. So, we went to the hill together where we planned to put up the cable car. We sat down, looked up the hill and developed ideas together – over the course of hours. We visualized it so intensely; it was as if the cable car was already there. We also went into details – like the color and design. At some point the Arab businessman looked at me, totally satisfied, and said, "You see, that's exactly the kind of cable car I want!"* – **Austrian businessman, Branch: Construction.**

What you need to understand: In the Arab business world, inquiring is based, as we saw in the previous case study, on a kind of brainstorming session. Both sides arrive at a mutual decision through a game of "question-answer-question." And it was definitely the inquiring that helped the international businessman find out the true wishes and desires of his Arab counterpart and understand what he really wanted. Especially in times of financial barriers in the Gulf, local business people will only carry out projects they are genuinely and personally convinced will succeed.

The Arab Business Code (ABC): You have to want to understand your Arab partner! And here I'm underlining the word "want," as so often before, because this attitude of "wanting" must be your honest, inner belief. Only then can you ultimately be successful in the Gulf. Of this I am sure, because Arab business people are very good at "hearing" what has been left unsaid in your mind (see Chapter 4.1). That's why Arab business people see projects they've been talked into as a personal insult. Here, you should not underestimate the perceptions of Arab business people. And this can have extremely negative side effects on your business together. In the worst case your Arab partner will call off the project.

But It's not enough to want to understand your counterpart, the honest intention to serve your counterpart has to be a priority. Again, there needs to be an honest intention to "serve." That has to be your priority. Therefore, pose one question to yourself and to your counterpart: "How can I support my Arab business partner." This total commitment will naturally be sensed by your business partner.

This is what Arab business people say:

> *Yes, when you sit with people, you can see how serious they act. Especially how they get back to you and what they ask.* – **Ahmed Hassan Bilal, prominent Qatari Businessman. Branch: Real Estate, Hospitality, Media.**

Successfully carrying out projects in the millions, by asking questions

Even with multi-million dollar projects, this technique is very effective. It helps to evaluate the strengths and weaknesses of the employees of the Arab companies you are working with, from the very beginning.

CASE-STUDY: Try to "really understand" the company

This is what international business people say:

> *When I work with a local company in Saudi Arabia, I try to really understand them. I go in there, check out everyone from the doorman to the top manager. I walk through all the levels – as far as that's possible. I certainly don't just hang around with the management: I try to really understand the company. With this philosophy, we successfully positioned ourselves into a billion euro project. And we developed the following strategies: we began to prepare the project half a year before it began, and we sat down with our Arab employees to conduct an intensive workshop. We sat together for hours and, after the workshop was over, we knew just how far we could go with our Saudi Arabian employees, exactly how much they would be able to achieve. Then we said, "Okay, we need to do the rest." And then everything worked out well.* – **Werner Piefer, German businessman. Branch: Safety Technology.**

What you need to know: This businessman goes the extra mile by taking it a step further when it comes to service, and ultimately benefits from it.

It's clear: when you know the other's limits and understand what the other side is, and is not, capable of, only then can you have successful teamwork. For this you need to analyze the weaknesses of the local employees and help them do what is needed. In your cooperation with the Arab partner you should see yourself, not only as a client or contractor, but as the director of your own film – with the title *Business Success in the Arab Gulf*. And for this, your "film," you will not only write your own screenplay, you will also act as your own casting director. Because it's not enough to understand your Arab business partner – you need to understand the whole team. Therefore, you need to find out if the local company's employees can even fulfill certain tasks. Keeping with the film business metaphor: directors need to know if their actors can really play their roles. Maybe their performances are even so spectacular that you, the director, will get an award for this film!

My tip: Sensitivity is required when dealing with the strengths and weaknesses of Arab employees. Always maintain a balance – showing the right degree of appreciation and sensing, at an early stage, when to be diplomatic or when to show them the right degree of appreciation.

CHAPTER 6

Conclusion
the commitment

In this last chapter I'd like to point out one main aspect that rises above all the other aspects, and it's probably the most important element: the commitment.

International companies must make an active and serious decision to work in the Arab Gulf and with its people. It means reaching an agreement with oneself: "Yes, I want to operate in this market, and yes, I want to do everything possible to ensure the cooperation with my Arab business partner is successful!"

Make your decision! People who are committed will notice ideas just pour out of them. You can share these brainstorms with your Arab counterpart to let him know you are really interested in building a successful future together, because you've made the decision – you've committed yourself.

Let us look at a few examples of how international business people present their commitment to their Arab business partners and which approaches they use. Here are some key messages describing the philosophy of people in the Gulf.

Commitment 1: "We give something back to the country!"

At this point, the classical Arab philosophy of "balance" is in the foreground; there must always be the same amount of give and take. And it's not about greed or getting rich. It's about creating something together from which a wider circle can profit – ideally, the whole country.

This is what Arab business people say:

Procter & Gamble, and Bechtel Corporation are good examples, or General Electric – from the beginning they concentrated on training Saudis, to educate them. These companies made a difference and got

very successful. Today we see them as a part of our country's growth.
**– Dr. Abdulrahman Alzamil, prominent Saudi Arabian busi-
nessman of a big family business, active in diverse areas.**

There are also further case studies of international business people
where considerations were made of what was necessary in the Gulf
States, what international companies needed to do to bring themselves into the right position and gain a foothold in the market there.
I'm thinking of a company that came to Saudi Arabia with thirty to
forty employees. This was a huge capital expenditure. At the same
time, including local employees in the project was encouraged, so they
invested in training and hired locals.

Some corporations even took it a step further and worked as companies with local staff at all levels – in the service and repair branches,
as well as in production. These companies made a name for themselves
across the entire Gulf region and were considered successful models,
internationally and by the locals.

What you need to know: "Nationalization" is an expression used by
certain Gulf States to describe the practice of employing locals. It is
known as Saudization, Qatarization, Emiratization etc., and will certainly continue to develop over the coming years. That's the government's clear goal. Accordingly, companies need to adjust to this and
work out appropriate strategies.

Try this: Think of how you can show your appreciation of the Gulf
States, to prove you want to work with them on a long-term basis. You
also want to earn money with these Gulf States, right? So, ask yourself:
what can we do for the Gulf States? Come up with ideas on how to create opportunities in knowledge transfer. Maybe you can instruct local
specialists, do onsite assembly, or even shift a part of the production
to the Gulf. Actions like these prove to your partners that you are committed. And this commitment will surely be rewarded. Don't forget,
the "archiving system" is active all the time, Arab business people in
the Gulf have long memories.

**Commitment 2: "We recognize the additional needs of the Arab
partners and help them!"**

Through these actions, you take on the important role of a "strategist"
regarding your partner. The goal is to achieve success by joining forces,
combining your strengths. Each profits from the other, and you strike
a balance.

CASE STUDY: *No delivery problems*

This is what international business people say:

> *We had a meeting with our Saudi Arabian partner. I already knew him very well, knew what he could achieve, because I had studied his company very carefully. In this meeting he suggested we try a different branch of business. I listened to him calmly, but I knew he couldn't meet the requirements of this sector. It was clear to me that we'd be headed for disaster with this. Maybe I could deliver and he couldn't, or he would deliver parts that didn't fit with mine. And then the day will come when people start to ask: "Why haven't you delivered this?" That would lead to fatal consequences, my partner would "lose face" because he couldn't provide the right service or supply the right thing. If this continued, it would one day cause an irreparable situation between us. All of this I knew. That's why I convinced my partner at this meeting not to take that step. And to keep on concentrating on our main area of business.* – **German businessman, active in diverse fields.**

What you need to understand: What makes this case study so unique is how forward thinking the international businessman is. And how diplomatically he deals with this situation. He takes over the responsibility for his Arab business partner. By doing this, he is behaving in accordance with the Arab Business Code – not only looking out for himself, but also considering the best interests of his counterpart.

Commitment 3: "Our philosophies, products and services fit one hundred per cent!"

International business people should always keep in mind that people in the Gulf have had decades of bad experiences in working together with international partners, with the delivery of poor quality and overcharging. This has broken the trust of Arab business people. That's why today's international business people need to prove the exact opposite. They need to be trustworthy.

CASE STUDY: *Car repair in Europe*

This is what international business people say:

> *We were supposed to deliver parts to an Arab businessman. But suddenly, huge technical problems popped up, because we couldn't*

produce the parts ourselves. On top of this, the subcontractor, an Italian supplier, had gone bankrupt. That was the moment we said: "Oh my God, that's it! What do we do now?" But then we made a decision: despite the high additional costs, which we had to pay out of our own pocket, we brought the car, on our own, to Europe and repaired it there. We got the vehicle into perfect working condition. We even explicitly invited our customer to pick up the car. As I said, all this we did for free, and it cost us a lot – but we still did it.

A little while later, we were called to a meeting and the Arab General Manager said to us: "This has never happened to us before! It's so unusual!" He continued telling us how much he appreciated the gesture. And that we would see the results of this in the future. At the time, we thought that was just a normal way of saying thank you. But from then on, all this company's tenders had one line with the following specifications: "We need so and so many vehicles with the specification number X." And this specific number was always accompanied with the name of our company. So, even now, many different companies can still supply specific parts for these cars, but it always has to be our cars they provide. The cars need to be purchased from us, to this very day. – **Austrian businessman. Branch: Special Vehicles.**

That's loyalty in the Gulf. People here notice when they are being treated well. And they will respond through their actions and reactions. Locals from the Gulf do not forget anything. As we have already seen – the Arab archiving code is active 24 hours a day, 365 days a year, and keeps track of everything to the smallest detail.

Commitment 4: "We invest enough time!"

This is what international business people say:

Besides the external sales, the biggest problem for the success of a project in the Arab Gulf is keeping the decision makers back home on board with the project; to motivate them to believe it makes sense to continue working on markets in the Gulf. – **Werner Piefer, German businessman. Branch: Safety Technology.**

Call to action: This businessman is addressing a significant problem here. My appeal to all owners and decision makers of international companies is to allow your employees the time they need to build up relationships with their Arab partners. These people have enough to worry about, without constant pressure and questions like: "Are you there yet? You've already been at it a year, when is the contract finally going to be signed?" Rushing things is very counterproductive in the Gulf. Please – and I'd like to stress this again, as a final point – give your employees time to form a relationship with the Arab business partner! Rome was not built in a day. Success and beauty take time. The same goes for business success in the Arab Gulf.

Keep that in mind! I wish you the best – from the bottom of my heart!

Yours, Judith Hornok

Appendix

MORE ON THE SEVEN EMOTIONAL HINDERERS

In various situations and encounters with Arab business people, Emotional Hinderers can manipulate people while doing business in the Gulf.

Here's a list of these creatures and where to find them in the book:

Frustrated Expectation

To expect something to happen, to anticipate a happy outcome, can be a wonderful and motivating feeling.

This is not the kind of expectation I'm talking about here. What I'm referring to is the frustrated form that has a destructive effect on people. Where anger and disappointment surface because the desired, intended, hoped for, or assumed actions and reactions have not happened.

In business cooperation with Arab business people in the Gulf, a frustrated form of expectation can cause serious long-term damage.

That's why I've devoted an entire chapter to the subject of managing your expectations.

You will find the Frustrated Expectation character in action on page 15.

Incensed Anger Rascal

Anger can also be a driving force. It releases energy and stimulates processes of change. Anger forces us to look for solutions to problems. We must let off steam somehow. Thus anger, applied in the right way, can be a fantastic way to generate new ideas and results. Here, I'm thinking of artists who express their anger by incorporating it into their creative process.

The Incensed Anger Rascal also has these capabilities, but unfortunately hasn't recognized them yet. Of this I am personally convinced –

you can use all seven members of the gang of Emotional Hinderers to your advantage. You just need to deal with them correctly.

Unfortunately, the Incensed Anger Rascal, only knows one form of expression – comparable to a volcano shortly before it erupts. It will use any and all means, to provoke volcanic emotional outbursts among the international business partners who feel offended, misunderstood or undervalued by their Arab counterparts. Regrettably, the Incensed Anger Rascal often steps into action here.

You will find a few examples on pages 15, 52, 71, 103, 125 and 126.

Relentless Judgment

The Relentless Judgment character is often not recognized as a serious disease, and the first symptoms are hard to spot. It's a gradual process that slowly gathers more strength, and moves in on you, because it's easier to repeat preconceived notions and opinions without checking them out first. Many people's laziness simply provides fertile ground for Relentless Judgment.

The Relentless Judgment character flourishes in the opinions of others, the group dynamics, our sense of belonging.

Something that all Emotional Hinderers like to do among themselves is seek each other's approval – making "the gang" stronger. Convincing each other to be right. But can you really trust statements made by third parties, even if they are in the majority?

The Relentless Judgment character doesn't care about this, because it doesn't accept any kind of criticism.

So, beware! The Relentless Judgment character can be extremely damaging to business in the Gulf. On the following pages are a few examples: 19, 20, 56, and 157.

Aggressive Inner Critic

Well balanced, the inner critic is a great protective mechanism. It cautions us to be critical of the actions and reactions of our Arab business partners and to carefully rethink the situation.

Hence, a "balanced inner critic" helps us get to know the locals better. Thus, enabling better access to them. This is helpful and extremely productive.

The difficulties lie in its aggressive expression. That's when the Aggressive Inner Critic becomes counterproductive.

The following pages exemplify this: 25, 190 and 191.

Insatiable Greed

Being curious about something new stimulates our spirit and creativity. But here we are talking about an aggressive hunger, in the form of Insatiable Greed.

It's hard to resist the Insatiable Greed character. The notion of getting something fast – money, power, prestige – is tempting.

The Insatiable Greed character lures international business people into being careless. You miss red flags, do not check the facts, because you've fallen in love with an idea (how you picture something) – of how perfect it could be.

Many business people know the situation where the Insatiable Greed character has bewitched them with seductive words: "Go for this project! Even if you don't have the resources now! Don't miss out on this opportunity. It'll work out in the end! Do not worry!" The Insatiable Greed character is dangerous company and needs to be recognized and confronted early on.

Here you will find situations of the Insatiable Greed character in encounters between international and Arab business people: page 49.

Paralyzing Fear

In principle, fear is a good warning signal that should be heeded. It makes us alert and reactive.

It's only dangerous if you become involved in a nagging inner conversation with yourself. When it paralyzes you before you even step into the conference room. When your thoughts start spinning. And the Paralyzing Fear character shouts at you: "You're not up to this! You will fail!" That's the moment when things begin to fall apart. Then you can be sure the Paralyzing Fear character has set in and is beginning to manipulate you.

Be aware of the Paralyzing Fear character! On page 79 of this book is an example of this.

Bloated Ego

A healthy ego is not only vital to our survival, but also enriches our lives.

I wouldn't like to imagine celebrities like Mick Jagger on stage with a weak ego. These glamorous, ego driven people inspire and motivate us. Healthy egotists are role models in our society.

It only gets difficult when the ego gets out of control and becomes more and more bloated – Me! Me! Me! That's when international business people totally lose their grip on reality regarding their local counterparts. Then, the Bloated Ego becomes a "crime scene" in dealings with Arab businessmen, a place where bad things can happen.

Also, in dealings with locals in the Gulf, the Bloated Ego can be extremely damaging to business.

One such example can be found on pages 156 and 157.

As tenacious as the characters of the Emotional Hinderers in business life in the Gulf are, you too should be determined to find new ways to control these creatures. Only then are you able to realize a long-term successful relationship.

I've talked to psychiatrists, psychologists, brain researchers, and many other experts about managing these creatures, decoding their behavior. And I have put together some useful tips for you, a collection of remarkable expert tips and techniques.

The time has come to apply our knowledge about Emotional Hinderers, to be aware of them, and benefit from the lessons they teach us.

In the future, I will dedicate my time more intensively to the "gang" of Emotional Hinderers. They are a family and belong together.

For more, see my website: www.judithhornok.com

Acknowledgments

This too – my second book – would not have come about without the help of many hard-working, enthusiastic "hands and heads," contributing knowhow, suggestions, inspiration and new approaches. A big thank you to all of you who motivated me to keep going. Because, again and again, I sensed the Aggressive Inner Critic, whispering in my ear reasons I should give up. But this creature was silenced by the words of one man: Senator Prof. Rudolf Öhlinger, a successful Austrian businessman and visionary. Dear Rudi, thank you for always believing in me. You were my backbone and will be for the rest of my life. Forever and ever. I'm already looking forward to working on the next book with you!

I thank my father and mother, for being the best parents – just the way they are! My gratitude and greatest appreciation go to my friend and colleague Sonja Ohly, who in our workshops not only impressively mimes the "Arab business partner" (Sonja, the world has lost a great actress in you) but also inspires me to new innovative approaches. Sonja – "never change a winning team!" Because we are simply there for each other in every way! Thanks also goes out to my business partner, Dr. Christian Baillou, who has loyally stood by me since the establishment of Hornok & Partner. Dear Christian, it's an honor to call you my business partner!

I also thank the "Editing Dream Team" revolving around Jonathan Griffiths, an experienced English-speaking publishing manager, who has supported me, for many years, with excellent tips and valuable suggestions. Ida Cerne, who not only spurred me on to develop the "Emotional Hinderers" but also worked on the English translation of this book. My illustrator Karen Jiyun Sung, and photographer Frank Helmrich, who is responsible for the artistic treatment of the silver case on the cover of this book. I am grateful to you all!

Special thanks go to Kristina Abbotts, without whom I wouldn't have found the way to Routledge. Also, thanks to the Routledge Editorial Power Duo, Amy Laurens and Alex Atkinson, and Tom Cole and Philip Stirups, whose tireless efforts and flexibility impressed me every day. Thank you so much! And not to be forgotten, my three musketeers: Hetti Bauer, Intisar Al-Yamani, and Karima Saini – the good and the loyal– all our conversations greatly inspired me to write this book. Thank you!

Finally, my gratitude goes to all the people who have accompanied me on this journey, over the course of many years, and placed their trust in me. Because without trust, no relationship will flourish. I thank you all, as well as my angels and Anna.

Yours truly, Judith

About Judith Hornok

Judith Hornok is the decoder and the founder of Hornok & Partner, an internationally recognized innovations company for business success in the Arab Gulf. Over the years, she has worked as a journalist for many leading publishers in Europe and the Middle East, writing about people and business, as well as producing TV documentaries such as, *The Makers Behind the Stars – The Man Behind Michael Schumacher*. She is the author of the book *Modern Arab Women*, in which she decoded "the quiet reformers." The book is featured in the Library of Congress in Washington, D.C. While writing *The Arab Business Code* she created the figures of the Emotional Hinderers.

Judith is famous for her lectures, including, among others, at IDEO/Stanford University and the European Forum Alpbach. She spends her time traveling between Europe, the US, and the Arab World.

For over fifteen years she has been studying the makeup and codes of business people in the Arab Gulf. She is convinced that only by speaking the "socio-emotional language" of these people and understanding their true motivations can one conduct successful business in the Gulf. With her team of experts, she has constant exchanges with psychiatrists, legal consultants, and Arab business people. Together they develop vigorous communications techniques and new approaches to help top managers and business people sensitize their perceptions about Arab counterparts – with the goal of targeting success by steering their talks and negotiations in a positive direction.

Since 2009 Judith has, together with her team, been imparting her knowledge to business people and employees of companies in individual training sessions and workshops. Among the clients of Hornok & Partner are numerous institutions, such as international trade organizations.